BEAR BRYANT
ON
WINNING FOOTBALL

BEAR BRYANT
ON
WINNING FOOTBALL

Paul "Bear" Bryant

Revised and updated by
GENE STALLINGS

PRENTICE-HALL, INC.   ENGLEWOOD CLIFFS, NEW JERSEY

Prentice-Hall International, Inc., *London*
Prentice-Hall of Australia, Pty. Ltd., *Sydney*
Prentice-Hall of Canada, Inc., *Toronto*
Prentice-Hall of India Private Ltd., *New Delhi*
Prentice-Hall of Japan, Inc., *Tokyo*
Prentice-Hall of Southeast Asia Pte. Ltd., *Singapore*
Whitehall Books, Ltd., *Wellington, New Zealand*

Originally published as
Building a Championship Football Team

Library of Congress Cataloging in Publication Data

Bryant, Paul W.
  Bear Bryant on winning football.

  Rev. ed. of: Building a championship football team.
[1960]
  Includes index.
  1. Football—Coaching. I. Stallings, Gene. II. Title.
GV956.6.B79 1983   796.332'07'7   83-112219
ISBN 0-13-071274-4
ISBN 0-13-071266-3 {PBK}

Printed in the United States of America

Bear Bryant Remembered

On December 15, 1982, when Paul W. "Bear" Bryant announced his retirement from coaching, surprise and dismay flowed through the coaching community and the country alike. Despite Bryant's age—69—few were prepared for the reality of a college football season without the "Bear's" awesome presence behind the Crimson Tide of Alabama.

The greatest shock came, however, only six weeks later when, on January 26, 1983, Bryant died suddenly of a massive heart attack following his hospitalization for chest pains the night before.

Coach Paul Bryant—college football's winningest coach—left behind a legacy measured not only in his career record of 323 wins, 85 losses and 17 ties. As eulogies were rushed into print, it became apparent that he also left behind a profound legacy of talent, toughness and humanity—both on the field and off—an overwhelming love of his sport and his players matched only by his ability to demand and receive the best from those around him.

From his players, in turn, he commanded love, respect, admiration and, frequently, an awe bordering on fear. Those who could live up to the Bear's high standards of performance, discipline and sheer hard work stayed with him. Those who could not, left. From the ranks of those who stayed over the years came more than 65 professional football players, including 44 head coaches at the college or professional level.

Paul William Bryant was born September 11, 1913, in Moro Bottom, Arkansas, the eleventh of 12 children of Wilson Monroe and Ida Bryant. His family worked a poor vegetable farm near Moro Creek and as a child he often accompanied his mother to Fordyce, eight miles away, to sell their produce. His father, a semi-invalid, was unable to contribute substantially to the family's support, and life was difficult.

7

Following her husband's death, Ida Bryant moved her family to Fordyce where prospects for the family's success seemed brighter. It was in Fordyce that the large, clumsy farmboy was spotted by the high school football coach, and Bryant began his playing career. It was also in Fordyce that he earned the nickname "Bear" by wrestling a muzzled carnival bear onstage for $1 a minute. It was a story he retold often in later years, including the fact that he momentarily pinned the bear and was holding on tight while the carnival master kept calling for action. Bryant usually added that for $1 a minute, he just wanted to keep the bear down forever! When the bear broke loose and the muzzle fell off, Bryant took off across the stage and out of the auditorium. He earned the nickname and several scars on his leg, but nothing else as the carnival left town before payment was made.

While playing for the Fordyce High School "Redbugs," Bryant was quickly spotted by scouts from the University of Alabama and recruited by the late Hank Crisp. He played a steady, competent game at Alabama, especially strong on defense, and became known as "the other end." He played flank opposite Don Hutson, one of the Crimson Tide's, and subsequently, pro football's greatest players. Both were on the 1934 Alabama team that defeated Stanford 29-13 in the Rose Bowl. Also that year, Bryant was named to the second team, All-Southeastern Conference.

In 1935, Bryant married Mary Harmon; the couple would have two children, Mae Martin and Paul Jr.

Bryant's talent in football lay in coaching. He began his career in 1936 following graduation from Alabama, staying on as an assistant coach at the request of head coach, Hank Crisp. Following three years at Alabama, he accepted the assistant coaching position under Red Sanders at Vanderbilt University. His dream of a career as head coach was interrupted by the start of World War II; he promptly volunteered to serve in the U.S. Navy.

Bryant attained the rank of Lieutenant Commander and served in North Africa but never was in any fighting. He was coaching pre-flight at Chapel Hill, North Carolina, when he returned to civilian life and began his head-coaching career.

Bryant's trip to the head-coaching job at Alabama was preceded by one year as head coach at Maryland, eight at Kentucky, and four at Texas A&M. When he returned to Alabama in 1958, it was the start of a 25-year head-coaching career there. In addition to winning 232 games for Bryant, the Crimson Tide won six national championships, 13 Southeastern Conference titles and played in 24 consecutive bowl games. Overall, Bryant coached 15 Conference championship teams (Kentucky won the SEC in 1950 and Texas A&M won the Southwest Championship in 1954) and participated in 29 bowl games.

In 1945, at the age of 32, Bryant became head football coach at the University of Maryland amid high hopes and enthusiastic support. Within a short time, however, the environment changed when Bryant found his authority undermined by the university president. Following two incidents—the president's firing of a Bryant assistant without telling him and reinstating a player that the head coach had dismissed from the team—Bryant knew he would have to resign. He did so, even though he had coached the Terrapins to a 6-2-1 record that year, including a win over Virginia, previously unbeaten in 16 games. The year before Bryant arrived, Maryland had won only one game.

Eight years in the head-coaching job at Kentucky followed. At Kentucky, Bryant finally had the chance to begin developing, over the long term, the tough, disciplined and demanding training program that his players would have to live with for the rest of his career. The program quickly paid off as, over the course of the years, the Kentucky football program grew in prominence and began to rival the well-known Kentucky basketball program of Adolph Rupp.

Over Bryant's eight seasons, the Kentucky Wildcats won 60 games, lost 23 and tied 5. The Wildcats had never been in a bowl game; under Bryant they went to the Great Lakes, Orange, Sugar and Cotton bowls. Kentucky also won the Southeastern Conference title in 1950, beating Oklahoma 13-7, thus ending the Sooner's 31-game winning streak.

Eventually, however, Bryant's success at Kentucky was the reason he had to quit. Kentucky was not big enough for a No. 1 football and a No. 1 basketball team; basketball had seniority. Although he had had a number of job offers over the years, the only head job open when he left Kentucky was at Texas A&M. There he experienced his only losing season as head coach, ending his first season with a 1-9 record.

This season at Texas A&M was made even more famous by the saga of the "Junction Boys." Upon arriving, Bryant took two busloads of his players to preseason practice in hot, dusty Junction, Texas. There—under the rigors of dawn-to-dusk training—the doors closed behind many a departing player. Bryant returned with less than half the team he started with!

Again, the efforts paid off, as the losing quickly ended and, after four years at the all-male, tradition-bound school, his record was 25-14-2. His third squad won the Southwestern Conference title in 1956, but was barred from the Cotton Bowl because of recruiting violations.

At Texas A&M, also, Bryant produced his only Heisman Trophy winner, John David Crow. Bryant's 1957 A&M team lost a disappointing Gator bowl to Tennessee, shortly after the formal announcement that Bryant had accepted the head coaching position back at the university where it all began over 20 years before.

One other nickname Bryant earned over the years was "The Great Rehabilitator." As he approached Alabama, his work was definitely cut out for him. The Crimson Tide had fallen on lean times, having won only three games in the three years before Bryant's arrival.

Bryant's first Alabama team won 5, lost 4 and tied 1. By the following season, with a record of 7-2-2, the Tide traveled to the Liberty Bowl, the first of 24 consecutive bowl trips. In 1961, following an undefeated and untied season, Bryant produced his first national championship team; he had two more undefeated/untied seasons and five more national championships at Alabama—the teams of 1964, 1965, 1973, 1978 and 1979.

Bryant's first years at Alabama were built around a defense that became a Tide trademark. In succeeding years he developed star runners who kept the offense mainly on the ground, and then passers who could keep an offense as wide open as necessary to beat any competition. With no offense, he would fall back on the quick defense and the kicking game, especially the quick kick.

The lack of size on his teams was no handicap to the Bear. He developed players who were lean and mean. The mid-sixties teams featured notable examples of starting linemen who weighed less than 200 pounds, several linebackers under 180 pounds and even several defensive backs in the 170 class.

By the end of the sixties, the Tide was on top and Bryant was the coach to beat. In the 60's the team had 90 wins, 16 losses and 4 ties, for the best record in the country.

The Tide rolled through the seventies, with an overall record surpassing that of the previous decade. From 1970 through 1979, it was 103 wins, 16 losses and 1 tie. Bryant was named National Coach of the Year three times—1961, 1971 and 1973. In 1981 he received his eighth award as SEC Coach of the Year, having won also in 1961, 1964, 1971, 1973, 1974, 1977 and 1979. No previous coach had won more than four times. In October, 1968, he was named the all-time Southeastern Conference coach by sports writers and editors.

In 1981 Bryant surpassed the previous record of 314 college wins of Amos Alonzo Stagg by winning game number 315 over Auburn, 28-17. Bryant accomplished this feat in 37 seasons, compared to Stagg's 57 seasons.

With his 38th season as head coach drawing to a close—and approaching the state's mandatory retirement age of 70—Bryant announced his retirement from coaching at a press conference on December 15, 1982. Several campaigns to waive the mandatory retirement law for Bryant had been started, but all without his endorsement, and in fact he opposed it. At his side for the announcement was his successor, protege, and former head coach of the New York Giants, Ray Perkins. As Bryant explained simply to the gathered reporters, he felt it was time for a younger man to take over.

One last game remained for the Bear—the Liberty Bowl in Memphis, December 29, 1982. Heavy media coverage was the order of the day as Bryant, wearing his famous houndstooth hat and eternal pokerface, coached his team to victory over Illinois, 21-15. Win Number 323 went into the record books.

At the time of his death in a Tuscaloosa hospital, Bryant still held the position of Athletic Director for Alabama, intending to relinquish it as soon as his coaching successor had comfortably settled in.

Tributes flowed into Alabama from all over the world as everyone—politicians, personalities, former and current players as well as the man on the street—tried to express what Bear Bryant and his legend at Alabama meant to them.

Many of the tributes were from "Bear's Boys"—his former players now active in many career fields as well as in the sports world. Although expressed in varying words, their eulogies were all similar. Bryant, the man and the coach, had challenged them all to be the best, to be No. 1. He was a man who hated to fail. His program of total dedication and devotion to football—the endless hard work to get it right—was aimed at developing champions for a lifetime, not just for a few hours on the gridiron.

Paul W. "Bear" Bryant, from Moro Bottom, Arkansas, left a legacy that will bear fruit for years to come.

TABLE OF CONTENTS

BEAR BRYANT
ON
WINNING FOOTBALL

CHAPTER 1

Why Football?

Have you ever wondered about football? Why it's only a game which is as fundamental as a ball and a helmet. But the sport is a game of great importance. If you take all of the ingredients that go into making up the game of football and put them into a jar, shake well and pour out, you've got a well-proportioned phase of the American way of life.

FOOTBALL IS MORE THAN A GAME

Football is the All-American and the scrub. It's the Rose Bowl with 102,000 cheering fans, and it's the ragged kids in a vacant lot using a dime-store ball. It's a field in Colorado ankle-deep in snow, and one in Florida sun-baked and shimmering.

Leaping cheerleaders, a brassy band, and the Dixie Darlings are a part of the wonderful game of football. It's a rich guy being chauffeured to the stadium gate, and a frightened boy shinnying the fence and darting for the end zone seats. It's a crowd which has gone crazy as it rips down the goal posts. And it's a nation stunned and wet-eyed at the news of Knute Rockne's death.

Football is drama, music, dignity, sorrow. It's exhilaration and shock. It is also humor and, at times, comedy. It's a referee sternly running the game. It's an inebriated character staggering onto the field and trying to get into the action.

Football is the memory of Red Grange, the Four Horsemen, and the Seven Blocks of Granite. It's a team's traditional battle cry, such as, "War Eagle," in the middle of the summer. It's a crisp fall day, traffic jams, portable radios and hip flasks. It's train trips, plane flights and victory celebrations. It's the losers moaning, "You were lucky, just wait'll next year!"

Names are football, such as Bronco, Dixie, Night Train, The Horse, Hopalong, Bad News, The Toe, and Mr. Outside.

FOOTBALL IS THE GREAT AMERICAN NOVEL

For four quarters, football is the Great American Novel, with chapters from Frank Merriwell, the Bible, Horatio Alger, the life of Lincoln and Jack the Giant-Killer.

Newspaper photos, arguments, Mr. Touchdown USA, yellowed clippings, the Hall of Fame, The Star-Spangled Banner—they're all football.

It's a game of young men with big shoulders and hard muscles. It's also a game of old pros, such as, 48-year-old George Blanda playing for the Oakland Raiders.

Football is popcorn, Cokes, banners and cigarette smoke. It's people standing for the kick-off, lap blankets, pacing coaches, penalties and melodious Alma Maters.

Football is a game of surprises. The big guy everybody picks in pre-season as All-American fizzles out. But a young man nobody every heard of scores the winning touchdown and a star is born. It's Tennessee going 17 games without being scored on. It's also tiny Chattanooga upsetting mighty Tennessee, making a coach's dream come true.

It's the pro halfback who is a movie star. And the water boy who got into a game at Yale. It's Bronco Nagurski butting down a sandbag abutment, and dwarfish Davey O'Brien disappearing from sight behind an array of 280-pound linemen. It's Harry Gilmer jumping high to pass, and Coach Vince Dooley proving that nice guys finish first.

Football is Paul Bryant, whose Alabama team is 40 points ahead, walking up and down the sideline like a caged lion. It's 35-year-old Danny Ford and 90-year-old Amos Alonzo Stagg. It's 6'9" Ed "Too Tall" Jones and 5'6" Eddie LeBaron.

Women who don't know a quick kick from a winged-T cheer every move on the field, waving pennants, purses and even mink stoles. That's football. So is the pressbox with it's battery of clattering typewriters. And the oldtimer who claims they played a better game in his day is a part of football, too.

It's Ray Berry, who wears contact lenses, making unbelievable catches for the Baltimore Colts. And after the game, when he dons his thick glasses, he looks the part of studious school teacher.

It's a scramble for tickets, playing parlays, wide-eyed youngsters getting autographs, a fist fight in the stands, second-guessing, banquets, icy rains, color guards, fumbles, goal-line stands, homecoming queens, and the typical mutt running onto the field attracting everyone's attention.

Football is Tommy Lewis jumping off the bench in the Cotton Bowl game and tackling a touchdown-bound Rice runner simply because, "I've got too much Alabama in me, I guess." It's the quivering voice of a dying George Gipp telling his Notre Dame teammates, "Win one for the Gipper."

It's New Year's, Christmas and the Fourth of July rolled into one. It's VJ Day, the Declaration of Independence, Haley's comet and Bunker Hill. It's tears and laughter, pathos and exuberance.

Football is a game that separates the men from the boys, but also it's a game that makes kids of us all.

Most of all it's a capsule of this great country itself.*

FOOTBALL IS THE AMERICAN WAY OF LIFE

Football, in its rightful place, can be one of the most wholesome, exciting and valuable activities in which our youth participate. It is the only sport I know of that teaches men to have complete control of themselves, to gain self-respect, give forth a tremendous effort and at the same time learn to observe the rules of the game, regard the rights of others and stay within bounds dictated by decency and sportsmanship.

Football, in reality, is very much the American way of life. As in life, the players are faced with challenges and they have an opportunity to match skills, strength, poise and determination against each other. The participants learn to cooperate, associate, depend upon, and work with other people. They have a great opportunity to learn that if they are willing to work, strive harder when tired, look people in the eye, and rise to the occasion when opportunity presents itself, they can leave the game with strong self-assurance, which is so vitally important in all phases of life. At the

*The author extends sincerest thanks to Clettus Atkinson, Assistant Sports Editor, *Birmingham Post-Herald*, for contributing this fine depiction of the meaning of football.

same time they are developing these priceless characteristics, they get to play and enjoy fellowship with the finest grade and quality of present day American youth.

The Game's Intrinsic Values

Not only is football a great and worthwhile sport because it teaches fair play and discipline, but it also teaches the number one way of American life—to win. We are living in an era where all our sympathy and interest go to the person who is the winner. In order to stay abreast with the best, we, also, must win. The most advantageous and serviceable lesson that we can derive from football is the intrinsic value of winning. It is not the mere winning of the game, but it is teaching the boys to win the hectic battle over themselves that is important. Sure, winning the game is important, and I would be the last to say that it wasn't, but helping a young man to develop his poise and confidence, pride in himself and his undertakings, teaching him to give that little effort are the real objectives of teaching winning football.

If I had my choice of either winning the game or winning the faith of a young man, I would choose the latter. There is no greater reward for a coach than to see his players achieve their goals in life and to know he had some small part in the success of the young men's endeavors.

Young men who participate in football, whether in high school or college, are in their formative years. It is every coach's responsibility to see that each young man receives the necessary guidance and attention he deserves. I would be deeply hurt and embarrassed if I learned a young man wasn't just a little better person after having played under my guidance. If we, as coaches, lose the true sense of the value of football and get to a point where we cannot contribute to a young man's progressing spiritually, mentally, and physically, we will be doing their wonderful game of football a great injustice by remaining in coaching.

The coaching profession is honorable and dignified and we football coaches are in a position to contribute to the mental development and desirable attitudes which will remain with the young men throughout their lives. We have the opportunities to teach intangible lessons to our players that will be priceless to them in future years. We are in a position to teach these young men intrinsic values that cannot be learned at home, church, school or any place outside of the athletic field. Briefly, these intangible attributes are as follows: (1) discipline, sacrifice, work, fight, and teamwork; (2) to learn how to take your "licks," and yet fight back; (3) to be so tired you think you are going to die, but instead of quitting you somehow learn to fight a little harder; (4) when your team is behind, you learn to "suck up your guts" and do whatever it takes to catch up and win the game; and (5) you learn to believe in yourself because you know how to rise to the occasion, and you know you will do it! The last trait is the most important one.

The Greatest Display of Courage

One personal reference will illustrate the intangible attributes that football teaches. We have all seen or heard someone tell about the greatest display of courage a team has ever shown. When a team you coach has had such an experience, it makes you exceedingly happy and proud of your position and the team. While I have never been ashamed of any of my football clubs, I will always have a soft spot in my heart for one of my teams in particular. I think my 1955 Texas A&M team displayed the greatest courage, rose to the occasion better, and did more of what I call "sucking up their guts and doing what was required of them" in a particular game than any other team with which I've ever been associated.

We were playing Rice Institute in Houston on a hot, humid afternoon. Our play was very sluggish and before we fully realized it, the game was almost over, and we were behind 12-0. We were leading the Conference race up to this point, but it was beginning to look as if we were going to be humiliated before 68,000 people. Having become disgusted with my starting unit's ineffective play, I withdrew the regulars from the game early in the fourth quarter. With approximately four minutes left to play, I decided to send the regulars back in. I told them they still had time to win the game if it meant enough to them to do so.

The first unit went onto the field and immediately called time out. I later found out they vowed to each other they were going to do whatever it took to win the game. We eventually got possession of the football on our own 42-yard line, and the clock showed 2:56 remaining to play. Again the boys called time out, giving each man a few seconds to make up his mind just exactly what he was going to do. On the first play from scrimmage, Lloyd Taylor, a little half-back from Roswell, New Mexico, ran 58 yards around left end for a touchdown. He kicked the extra point and the score was 12-7, with 2:08 remaining in the game. We tried an on-side (short) kick, and Gene Stallings recovered the ball on Rice's 49-yard line. Our quarterback, Jimmy Wright, then threw a 49-yard pass to Lloyd Taylor who made a beautiful catch as he crossed the goal line. Taylor scored his fourteenth point as he kicked his second point-after-touchdown placement. With the score 14-12, we lined up and kicked the ball deep to Rice. Forced to gamble since they were behind, Rice attempted a deep pass which our great fullback, Jack Pardee, intercepted and returned 40 yards to the 3-yard line. On the next play Don Watson carried the ball across for a touchdown, making the final score 20-12 in our favor.

After the game in our dressing room, when everyone was congratulating each other and everything was in a state of confusion, Lloyd Taylor suggested we thank the Master for giving us the courage to make the great comeback. From that game on we have always said a prayer of gratitude after the game, win, lose, or draw.

The particular incident cited was the greatest display I have ever seen of young men reaching back and getting that little extra, showing their true colors, and rising to the occasion and putting into practice the thing that we preach and believe in.

What do we get out of coaching? There is nothing in the world I would swap for the associations with those young men, and the other fine men I have coached, and the self-satisfaction of knowing I've helped many young men to find themselves. In my estimation, football is truly a way of life.

CHAPTER 2

The Theory of
Winning Football

Every football team has a slogan, and each coach has his own theory as to what makes a winning team. We are no exception. Our slogan is, "Winning is not everything, but it sure beats anything that comes in second." Our theory of how to develop a winning team is very simple—WORK! If the coaches and players will work hard, then winning will be the result.

We want to win. We play to win. We are going to encourage, insist and demand that our players give a 100 percent effort in trying to win. Otherwise we would be doing them a great injustice. It is very important for young men to have a complete understanding of what they must do in order to win.

When a young man has completed his eligibility or has played four years under our guidance, I like to believe he will graduate knowing how to suck up his guts and rise to the occasion, and do whatever is required of him to get his job done. If our young men are willing to work hard, and we give them the proper leadership and guidance, then they will graduate winners and our athletic program will be a success.

HOW TO START BUILDING A WINNER

Building a winning football team is something that cannot be accomplished overnight, or even in a year or two, if the program is starting from scratch. I believe, regardless of the time element in-

volved, a football program has little chance of succeeding unless the
following "musts" are adhered to:

1. The coach must have a definite plan in which he believes, and there must be no compromise on his part.
2. The football coach must have the complete cooperation
   and support of the administrators and the administration,
   who must believe in the head coach, his staff, and his
   plan.
3. The coach must have a long-term contract.
4. The coach must not only be dedicated to football, but he
   must be tough mentally.
5. The head coach must have the sole responsibility and
   authority of selecting his staff of dedicated men, who
   must believe in the head coach and his plan.

The Administration Must Believe in Your Plan

It is vitally important that a coach build a solid foundation for
his program. In order to do this he must have complete cooperation
from every member of the school's administration. In many cases,
the school officials will not have a complete and thorough understanding of your athletic program. It is important that you explain to
them just what you are trying to accomplish, how long it will take,
and why you are doing it in your particular manner. The administrators and the administration must understand the value the program has for each young man who participates, and the ways the
program can benefit the entire school system. Therefore, before a
coach accepts a particular position he should give considerable
thought to the administration's philosophy, attitude or point-of-view
toward the football program. If the school president or principal is
skeptical, consider the position seriously before accepting it. Building a championship team is difficult enough with full cooperation
from everyone, but it is an impossible coaching situation without the
administration's full support and confidence.

The Coach Must Have a Long-Term Contract

If a college coach is going to build a team, it is an absolute
must that he have a long-term contract. There is little use in believ-

ing or thinking any other way. It is quite possible, and highly probable, it will take at least four or five years to shape a ball club into winning form. Without the security of a long-term contract, a coach can be forced to concentrate on winning a certain number of games each year, and it is possible this can completely disrupt or disorganize a rebuilding program. I am not saying that a coach should not try to win every game, because he obviously should strive to win 'em all. I merely want to point out the fact that without the security of a job for a period of years, he might be forced to revert to certain practices which he knows are not sound principles on which to build a winning program. As an illustration, he might have to revert to such a practice as playing individuals of questionable character because of their immediate ability, rather than weeding them out and concentrating on the solid citizens. The latter group will stay with you and will eventually be winners, if you are given job security and adequate time to work with them.

The Coach Must Be Dedicated and Tough Mentally

Unless a person is dedicated to his chosen trade or profession, regardless of his field of endeavor, he is never going to be highly successful. Building a winning football team is no exception. The head coach, as well as his assistants, must be dedicated to football. All of them must be tough mentally, too.

Many times a coach's job is unpopular and unrewarding. From time to time a coach must make decisions that are unpleasant. He cannot compromise, however, if he expects to build a winner. He must be tough mentally in order to survive.

In addition, a coach must be tough mentally in another sense. He must be able to spend numerous hours studying football all ways and always. A coach who hopes to be successful must drive himself and be so dedicated to his job that he puts it ahead of everything else in his life, with the exception of his religion and his family. One can have a tremendous knowledge of the game, but he cannot possibly make the grade unless he can stand up to the long hours and the trying times. It is not an absolute necessity for a coach to be exceptionally smart or a brilliant strategist, but he must be a hard worker, mentally tough, and dedicated to the game of football. One can only be honest with himself in determining whether or not he has these qualifications.

You Must Have a Definite Plan

As head football coach, you must give leadership and direction to your program if you expect it to be successful. Therefore, you must have a definite plan in which you and your assistants believe. In order to build winners you cannot deviate from your plan, and there cannot be any compromises.

Many factors go into the plan, such as organizing the program and the type of young men whom you have on your squad, both of which will have a great deal to do with your ultimate success or failure. These and other phases of the plan will be discussed in detail shortly, and in later chapters in this book.

You Must Have a Good Staff

In order to build winners, the head coach must surround himself with a dedicated staff of hard-working coaches. While I have touched on this point briefly already, this particular must will be discussed in greater detail in Chapter 3, "Making the Most of Your Coaching Staff."

You Must Have the Ability to Adjust

The coach and his staff must have the ability to adjust with the times. Football changes and so do people. The successful coach is the one who sets the trend and not always the one who is following it. We've gone from the short punt to the Single Wing to the Split T to the I to the Wishbone to multiple formations with quite a lot of movement. The plays have also undergone some changes, and we must understand this, too, if we are going to be successful.

The influence of television, professional football and the "times" will make us all readjust our thinking process, even though our basic principles are the same.

THE TYPE OF PLAYER = SUCCESS OR FAILURE

The team with the best athletes will usually win the tough ball games, other things being equal. It is a well-recognized fact that a coach is no better than his material. Therefore, we must have the best material available in order to be a winner. I tell my coaches if they can recruit the best athletes to our school, then I can coach them. If they recruit mediocre athletes, then the assistants will have to coach them.

There are a number of qualifications that we look for in our athletes, and some of these are musts if the young men are to become champions. Football is nothing more than movement and contact. If a player has excellent movement but won't make contact, he will never be a winner. Conversely, if a player is tough, loves body contact, and likes to hit people, but is so slow he never gets to the ball carrier, then he will never make a winner either. There are ways to improve an individual's quickness, but if a player refuses to make contact, there is nothing that I know of to correct it.

The type of player you select to play on your football team has a great deal to do with your ultimate success or failure. In order for our program to be successful, we try to select the boy with the following traits:

1. He must be dedicated to the game of football.
2. He must have the desire to excel and to win.
3. He must be tough mentally and physically.
4. He must be willing to make personal sacrifices.
5. He must put team glory first in place of personal glorification.
6. He must be a leader of men both on and off the field.
7. He should be a good student.

The Players Must Be Dedicated

A player must be dedicated to the game to the extent he is willing to work, sacrifice, cooperate and do what he possibly can to aid the team in victory. It is our duty as coaches to explain and show our young men the advantages of being winners, and to impress upon them the absolute necessity for it so that they will put forth the much-needed effort to accomplish the objective. It is important for the players to understand that football is not an easy game; nor is achieving fame an easy task. However, anything worth doing, is worth doing right. Therefore, let's do it right and be winners.

We refer to "the little extras" a player must give in order to be a winner. These little extras really make the difference between good and great, whether it be on an individual or a team basis. When a player puts into practice what you have been preaching about giving that extra effort when he is dog-tired, going harder, rising to the occasion and doing what is necessary to win, then you are making progress and he is on the way to becoming a winner both individually and for his team.

There is nothing else I would rather see than when our men are in their goal-line defense, and they have supreme confidence they will keep the opposition from scoring. Every individual is taking it upon himself personally to do what is necessary to stop the ball carrier from scoring. When a coach has a team thinking like this, he will have a winner, and the men will be winners when they get out of school.

Our Players Must Have the Desire to Excel

We talk about the importance of particular aspects of coaching, such as full cooperation, long contracts, and other phases connected with coaching, but in the final analysis the success or failure of your program depends on the performance of the players on the playing field. The game is generally won by the men with the greatest desire. The difference in winning and losing is a very slight margin in a tough ball game. The same applies to two players of equal ability, except that one is great and the other is average. What is this slight margin? It's the second and third effort, both individually and as a team. The player who intercepts a pass or blocks a punt, or who gets his block then goes and knocks down another opponent is the individual who wants to excel. He will make the "big play" when it counts the most. He and others will give us "the winning edge." These are the deciding factors in a tough ball game.

You Must Beat Your Opponent Physically

The teams that win consistently are the ones in the best physical condition. As a result they can play better football than their opposition in the fourth quarter. We also believe and teach our players they must be more aggressive and "out-tough" our opponents if they expect to win consistently.

We may not be as smart and as tricky as our opposition, so we have to out-work 'em. If our players are in top physical condition, if we "out-tough" and physically whip our opponents by hard blocking and tackling, and we are consistent in doing it, we will win a lot of football games. Football is a contact sport, and we must make the initial contact. In order to be a winner, a player must whip his man individually, and the team must beat the opponent physically.

Genuine All-Out Desire for Team Victory

Unity is the sound basis for any successful organization, and a football team is no exception. Without team unity, you cannot have winners. We believe and coach team victory. Our goal is to win every game we play. We go into every game believing we will win it. Obviously we don't win all of them, but we never go into a game believing we cannot come out of it the winner.

In order to have a winner, the team must have a feeling of unity; every player must put the team first, ahead of personal glory. The men who play for us must be willing to make sacrifices. Victory means team glory for everyone. Individual personal glory means little if the team loses.

Must Be a Leader and a Good Student

In order to have winners, your players must be leaders both on and off the field. They should be good students, too. As was indicated previously, if your contract will give you sufficient time to work with the "solid citizens," they will stay with you even if the going gets tough, and eventually they will be winners.

You Can't See into the Heart of a Young Man

Most coaches take pride in their ability to pick out players with athletic ability. I am no exception. However, you can never be absolutely certain about an individual because you cannot see what is inside of his heart. If we could do this, we would never make a mistake on a football player. We have seen it occur frequently where a player was pitiful in his freshman year, and the coaches almost gave up on his ever improving. However, through determination, hard work, pride, and desire the boy would finally develop and would play a lot of football before he graduated.

One of my former assistant coaches, the late Carnie Laslie, had a favorite story he liked to tell about a player we had at the Univer-

sity of Kentucky. We had started our first practice session in the fall
of 1948 when a youngster walked out on the field. His appearance
literally stopped practice. He had on a zoot suit with the trouser legs
pegged so tightly I am certain he had difficulty squeezing his bare
feet through the narrow openings. His suspenders drew up his trous-
ers about six inches above his normal waist line. His long zoot coat
extended almost to his knees. His "duck tail" hair style looked
quite unusual. He was standing in a semi-slump, and twirling a long
chain around his finger when one of my assistants walked over and
asked him if he wanted someone. His answer, "Yeah. Where's the
Bear?"

He found me in a hurry. Our first impression was that he
would never be a football player, but he was issued a uniform
anyway. I figured he wouldn't have the heart for our type of football
and would eliminate himself quickly from the squad. To help him
make up his mind in a hurry, I instructed one of the coaches assist-
ing me to see that he got plenty of extra work after practice. The
boy's name was difficult to pronounce, so we started calling him
"Smitty."

Despite "Smitty's" outward appearance, he had the heart of a
competitor and the desire to show everyone he was a good football
player. He worked hard and proved his point. In his senior year, he
was selected the outstanding player in the 1951 Sugar Bowl game
when we defeated the University of Oklahoma. After graduation, he
played for several years with the New York Giants as a fine defensive end. I shall always have the greatest respect for him.

Other coaches probably have had similar experiences where a
young man with questionable ability has made good. If a player has
a great desire to play football, regardless of his ability, and you
work with him, he is likely to make tremendous progress toward
fulfilling his objective.

GOOD ORGANIZATION—A BIG FACTOR
IN BUILDING WINNERS

Without good organization our thoughts or plans of any kind
would be absolutely useless. Good organization is a must if a team
is to operate at maximum efficiency. There are many plans of organization that are good, and I am not saying mine is the best, but I
believe my plan is sound and this is what really counts.

It always has been my practice to observe people who are successful in a particular field, and try to determine what makes their operation successful. There is little originality remaining in the field of coaching. Consequently, we have gotten many of our ideas from other people. As Frank Howard, Athletic Director of Clemson University put it, "If we get something from one team, it's called stealing; but if we get ideas from several different teams, it's called research."

Use the Ant Plan

I borrowed my plan of organization from some ants in Africa. I realize this sounds ridiculous and far-fetched; nevertheless, it's the truth. It is interesting how it all came about.

While I was in the Navy in Africa, one hot, humid afternoon, I was sitting under a tree feeling sorry for myself. I started to watch some ants building an ant hill. At first I was amused, but as I watched, I became very interested. What at first appeared to be confusion was actually a carefully organized plan as the ants all worked toward their objective of building a home. The longer I watched the more obvious it became that all of the ants were working, many in small groups here and there. There was no inactivity, no wasted motion. There was unity and there was a plan. It appeared the ants had planned their work and they worked their plan.

With the ant plan in mind, we try to organize our practice sessions so that we have everyone working and no one standing around idle. We work in small groups and this eliminates inactivity. As a result, we feel that we can get more work done in a shorter period of time. Consequently, we believe the less time a player spends on the practice field, the higher will be his morale.

I did not have to watch the ants to learn the value of teamwork and cooperation, although this was evident in their activity. The main lesson I learned from them was the value of small group work in order to keep everyone busy.

There are many other factors that must be taken into consideration when organizing the program, and I shall discuss the subject more fully in Chapters 3 and 10. Planning and organization are the backbone of a successful team. Planning a practice so that you get maximum results from the players and the assistant coaches requires a great deal of time. The importance of this cannot be emphasized too greatly.

CONCLUSION

Winning theories vary from coach to coach, but our philosophy toward building a winner consists of the following factors: (1) a hard working staff that is dedicated to football; (2) players with a genuine desire to excel, to "out-tough" the opponent, and be in top physical condition; (3) a strong organization and a sound plan; (4) mental toughness in both staff and players; and (5) the full confidence of the school administration. In addition, you must teach sound football. Your players and your staff must have confidence in your type of football. I shall discuss our methods fully in later chapters.

CHAPTER 3

Making the Most of the Coaching Staff

I AM A FIRM BELIEVER IN THE OLD SAYING, "A head coach is no stronger than his assistant coaches." In order for any head coach to have a good program, he must surround himself with a staff of good assistant coaches. This does not mean that every coach must have six or eight assistants. In some cases, the head coach may not have more than two or three assistants. The principles are the same, however, regardless of the number of assistant coaches. I have been fortunate in having an excellent group of assistants every place I have coached, and I want to give credit to them for any measure of coaching success I have had in the past.

ASSISTANT COACH: TYPE OF MAN

There are many characteristics I seek in an assistant coach. I shall not attempt to list them in the order of importance because I think they all belong at the top of the list. Briefly, the desirable traits and characteristics I am seeking in an assistant are as follows:

1. He should be dedicated to the game of football.
2. He should be willing to work hard and to make personal sacrifices.
3. He should be an honest person.
4. He should have a sound knowledge of football.
5. He should have a great deal of initiative.
6. He should be a sound thinker.
7. He should be tough mentally.

A Dedicated Person, Hard Worker, Loyal

The first trait, "Be dedicated to the game of football," is a must for all coaches, assistants as well as head coaches. Don't ever try to fool yourself or anyone else. If you are not truly dedicated to your work, and you dread spending many hours every day working and planning on building a good football team, then you are in the wrong business. I'll guarantee there is no easy way to develop a winning team. If it were an easy task, all of us would be undefeated and "Coach of the Year." Unfortunately, one team generally wins and the other loses, and if it is the latter it doesn't make a coach's job any easier. If you will look at the consistent winners, you will find behind them a group of coaches who are 100 percent dedicated to their work.

Regardless of whether it's the college or high school level of competition, there are coaches and teams that win year after year. The real reason for this success, other than good material, is the coaches of these particular teams are dedicated to the extent that they "want" to do what is necessary to win. There is a big difference between "wanting to" and "willing to" do something to be a winner. Frankly, I don't like the word "willing" in connection with an assistant coach. First, if the coaches are not willing, they should not be coaching. Coaching is not an 8 a.m. to 5 p.m. job. The assistant who is "willing" to work a little extra is not the one I want on my staff. The assistant who "wants" to do what is necessary in order to get the team ready to play, regardless of the time element involved, is the man I want to assist me.

A head coach cannot expect his assistants to be dedicated to their work, unless he leads by example. The head coach must work harder, longer, and be more dedicated to his work than any of his assistants, if he expects to have a good, hardworking staff and winners.

Another qualification I consider a must for all assistant coaches is their 100 percent loyalty to the head coach's plan. It is very important for a coach and his staff to know they have mutual trust in and loyalty to each other. These characteristics are obvious, and an assistant coach who does not possess them commits professional suicide.

Initiative and Ambition

An assistant coach should have a great deal of initiative and ambition. I prefer to have my assistants study the game all ways and always. They should constantly try to improve themselves. There is no corner on the brain market and a person advances in the field through hard work and his own initiative.

It is a must that all coaches be good "mixers." They must be able to get along with each other, the head coach, the players, and the people in the community. On the college level, a coach must know how to recruit, and most of the time the successful recruiter is a good mixer. He must sell your product—the school, the team, the coaching staff, etc.—to athletes and their parents, and his job will be easier if he has this type of personality.

Honesty and Integrity

It is an absolute must that all coaches be honest with themselves, the people for whom they work, and the others with whom they come in contact. If I cannot trust a person, I do not want him around. Along this same line, we like our coaches to be active in their church work. We emphasize to our players the value of attending church, and we like our coaches to set a good example for everyone.

A Sound Thinker with a Good Understanding of the Game

In order for a coach to be competent, he must be a sound thinker and possess a good knowledge of the game of football. I have mentioned this previously. I expect my assistants to study, plan, discuss and try to come up with ideas that might aid us in winning a football game. We are going to toss around all ideas in our staff meetings before we adopt any of them, but your brand of football can become stale and unprogressive if the coaches do not study the game.

DIVISION OF COACHING DUTIES

Morale on a squad is very important. The morale of a coaching staff is very important, too. I feel the latter group will influence the former group, consequently I am vitally concerned about my assistants having good morale. With this thought in mind, I try to delegate duties and responsibilities so the assistants enjoy their work. Each man is really a specialist, or he can do some phase a little better than another coach. Therefore it's just common sense to permit him to work at the specialty in which he is going to excel. He will not only have more enthusiasm for his work, but his enthusiasm will be reflected in the players' work. There is no substitute for enthusiasm. Under such conditions, the players learn more quickly and the coaches are able to do a better job of coaching.

Assistant Coaches Direct Group Work

I do not think it advisable for a head coach to do group work with one of his assistants. If an assistant is directing a group and the head man comes over to help out, he takes the lead away from the assistant. As a result the assistant coach is likely to lose his initiative—the very trait you want him to develop. Second, the players are likely to give the head coach all of their attention, and this isn't fair to the assistant working with the same group of young men. Third, I do not think it is desirable to suggest changes, make corrections or reprimand an assistant on the field. I feel the proper time to get the matter straightened out is after practice, and not while the players are around. I always try to avoid situations which are not conducive to good team and staff morale because you've got to have good morale in order to build a winner.

The Coaching Specialist

I think it is important for my assistants to specialize in either offensive or defensive football. I feel they can do a better job of coaching if they devote most of their time and effort toward one aspect or the other. We still want them to be cognizant of the opposite phase, however, as the defensive coaches must understand offensive football, and vice versa for the offensive coaches. In fact, from time to time, I will put an offensive coach with the defense so he can learn more about this particular phase of the game. I believe it would be advisable for a high school coach, with possibly only a staff of two, to follow the same plan—one offensive coach and the other on defense.

Immediately after practice every day during the season I meet with my staff. I have little patience with the assistant who wants to hurry away from practice immediately. I want my staff members to meet in the staff room so we can discuss all phases of the day's practice schedule while it is still fresh in our minds. Evaluation of personnel goes on all the time. Therefore, I want my assistants to list on the blackboard the work schedule for the next day for their particular group of men. In addition, I want their suggestions and comments as to the type of teamwork needed. Now I am in a better position to do a more intelligent job of setting up the practice schedule for the next day since I have been made aware of our individual and team needs, strengths, and weaknesses. We have found this procedure very helpful, and I encourage my assistants to express themselves. I shall explain our procedures more fully in Chapter 10.

Delegating Responsibility

The head coach must delegate responsibility to his assistants in order to have a more effective plan of operation. The head coach must let each assistant know what he expects from him. An explanation of duties and responsibilities in the beginning is likely to eliminate misunderstanding later on. Second, a person with some responsibility is likely to do a better job than the individual who doesn't have any. I have found it gives the assistant more confidence in himself and more pride in his work if he has been given a certain amount of responsibility.

As I mentioned previously in Chapter 2, in order to get the most from your staff, they must be completely sold on your plan for building a winner. Of course, the head coach must believe in his own plan 100 percent, along with the assistants, and he cannot make any compromises if he expects to be successful.

A Good Coach Is a Good Teacher

We stress the point frequently that coaching is teaching of the highest degree, and a good coach is a good teacher. It is not what you and your assistants know about football that is going to win the games, but rather what you are able to teach your players. In order to give our coaches an opportunity to improve their coaching techniques, we have them get up at staff meetings and explain and answer the questions to our satisfaction. We have found this method gives the coaches a lot of confidence and they do a better job of coaching on the field.

CONCLUSION

In order for the head coach to get the maximum from his assistants, he must set a good example. Since others will follow a leader who actually leads, rather than one who merely tells what to do, I believe a head coach must work longer, harder, and stay a jump ahead of his assistants and the other coaches in the profession. He must be dedicated to the game of football, well organized, sound in his thinking, and have the ability to delegate authority and responsibility to his assistants if he expects to build a successful program.

CHAPTER 4

Defense:

Our Kind of Football

W E BELIEVE DEFENSE IS ONE OF THE MOST IMPORTANT PHASES OF FOOTBALL. We feel if we do not permit the opposition to score, we will not lose the football game. While in reality most teams actually score on us, we still try to sell our players on the idea that if the opposition does not score, we will not lose.

If you expect to have a good defensive team, you must sell your players on the importance of defensive football. Our players are enthusiastic about defensive football. I believe we do a good job of teaching defensive football because the staff and players are sold on what we are trying to do. Defense is our kind of football.

DEFENSIVE OBJECTIVES

The primary objective of defensive football is to keep the opposition from scoring. We want our players to feel their ultimate objective is to keep the opposition from crossing our goal line.

A more functional facet of the primary object is to keep the opposition from scoring the "easy" touchdown, which is the cheap one, the long pass or the long run for six points. While a singular long run or a long completed pass may not actually defeat us, it is very likely that if either play breaks for the "easy" touchdown we will be defeated.

Second, our kicking game must be sound, which I shall discuss fully in Chapter 6. We must be able to kick the ball safely out of dangerous territory. Providing we do this, and eliminate the "easy" touchdown, we believe our opposition's own offense will stop itself 50 percent of the time through a broken signal, a penalty or some other offensive mistake. Therefore, if our players are aggressive while on defense, we will probably keep our opposition from scoring about 25 percent of the time they have the ball. The remaining 25 percent will be a dog fight. Therefore, we must instill in our defensive men a fierce competitive pride that each player is personally responsible for keeping the opposition from scoring.

The Offensive-Minded Defense

Our next objective is to sell the players on the idea our defensive unit can and will score for us. There are more ways to score while on defense than on offense; consequently, the odds favor the defense. If statistics are kept on the defensive team's performance, and the defensive team is given credit for all scores made by running back a punt, recovering a funble or any other defensive maneuver where they either score or get the ball for their offense inside the opposition's 25-yard line, which results in a score, the players can be sold on the idea of the offensive-minded defense.

Previously I mentioned the importance of good morale in building a winner. In order to sell a player on defense, you must create good morale. Therefore, we sell our men on the idea that playing defense is the toughest assignment in football. We try to see that our defensive players get most of the recognition and favorable publicity. If our defense makes a goal line stand, and we win the game, we try to give most of the credit to our defensive players.

Sell Them on Defensive Football

We want to make our defensive players believe that when the opposing team has the ball inside our 3-yard line they aren't going to score—they can't score—they must not score! If a team believes this, it's almost impossible for the offense to score. In 1950 our defensive unit prevented opposing teams from scoring on 19 occasions from the 3-yard line. Our 1961 Alabama team gave up 22 points all year and we had 5 shutouts. This team was one of the all-time greats on defense and it was captained by Lee Roy Jordan, who went on to be a great linebacker for the Dallas Cowboys. The morale of the defensive players was outstanding. They thought it was impossible for another team to score on them even though they had only three yards to defend. When I was coaching at Kentucky, in our game with Oklahoma in the Sugar Bowl, the Sooners got down to our 3-yard line. We had three or four of our best players on the bench, and I was trying to get them back into the game quickly. The late former head coach of Oklahoma, Jim McKenzie came off the field, and said, "Don't worry, Coach, they will never score on us." And they did not score! When I see such evidence, I know our players believe what we tell them.

Goal line defense has always been the heart and soul of a great team. Many great teams bend in the middle of the field, but refuse to break when the opponent gets inside the ten-yard line.

Two of our most meaningful goal line stands occurred against Penn State in the 1979 Sugar Bowl and the 1981 game in State College.

The Sugar Bowl goal line stand was with all of the marbles on the line. We were playing for the National Championship. The score was 14-7, Alabama, and our punter shanked a punt out of bounds on our own 31-yard line. One play later it was first and goal at our 8. The first play netted two. On second down Penn State threw a pass and Don McNeil made a game-saving tackle at the one. Our defense rose to the occasion on the next two Penn State rushes and we held on to win the game and the National Championship.

In State College, we had jumped out to a sizable lead in the first half. The first series of the third quarter is one of the most important in the game from the standpoint of momentum.

We kicked off and Penn State marched right down the field in ten plays to a first down at our four-yard line. What happened from there might be the best goal line defense that any of our teams ever played. We held them to two yards in two carries. On third down a pass interference call was made giving Penn State a first down at our one.

No one in the stadium thought we could stop them, except our eleven defensive players. With a great rushing team, Penn State rushed four straight times for no gain. We were able to take over, keep the momentum from turning around, and win the game. (It just so happened that that game was Coach Bryant's 314th win which tied him with Amos Alonzo Stagg as college football's Winningest

Coach.) Alabama held 7 straight downs inside the 4 to keep Penn State out of the end zone.

I do not believe you can teach defensive football successfully unless you are able to present a clear picture to your players of what you are trying to accomplish. Our objective is to limit the offense to as small an area as possible. By limiting their attack, we can hem them in and catch them. We attempt to build a fence around the ball, and around the offensive operation. I want my players to have a good picture of exactly how we are going to build this fence, and what we hope to accomplish, both of which will be explained later.

Defense Is a Personal Challenge

Defense is a phase of football I have always considered very interesting because every play is a personal challenge. When a team is on defense, the players are challenging the offensive players in relating to an area of ground or field. Every man on defense should believe, "I am not going to let the offense score." If you expect to be a winner, either as a player or a coach, you must believe in this philosophy 100 percent. Your play must be sound, and you must believe in it.

Offensive football is assignment football, while defense is reaction football. One mistake on defense can cost a team a football game. Consequently, there cannot be errors on defense. By being sound, and in order to eliminate errors, I mean you must always have the strength of your defense against the strength of the offense. The defensive players must be positioned in such a way that the team as a whole can handle any situation that might arise.

DEFENSIVE AXIOMS

There are numerous defensive alignments, just as there are different points-of-view or theories toward how defense should be played. Regardless of the differences and a coach's particular plan, the following "musts" are considered basic axioms if a defense is to be sound:

1. The defense must not allow the opponent to complete a long pass for an "easy" touchdown.

2. The defense must not allow the opponent to make a long run for an "easy" touchdown.
3. The defense must not allow the opposition to score by running from within your 5-yard line.
4. The defense must not allow the opposition to return a kick-off for a touchdown.
5. The defense must not allow the opposition to average more than 20 yards per kick-off return.
6. The defense must intercept one pass out of every 13 passes attempted.
7. The defense must average 20 yards per return on each interception.
8. The defense must return two interceptions for touchdowns per season.
9. The defense must force the opposition to fumble the ball on an average of three times per game.
10. The defense must recover an average of two fumbles per game.

These 10 basic axioms are extremely important, and must be applied if a team is to be sound defensively.

Defense—A Team Proposition

A good sound defense is one that has every player on defense carrying out his assignment. Then it is impossible for the offense to score. Note that I said every player, which makes defense a team proposition and eliminates the individual defensive play. By this I mean every defense is coordinated and a player just doesn't do what he wants to do. I do not mean suppressing an individual's initiative or desire to excel while on defense, as long as the entire defense is a coordinated unit. We try to instill in every young man that he is personally responsible to see that our opposition does not score. When individual players and a team accept this responsibility, I feel we are making progress and beginning to build a winner.

Gang Tackling—A Defensive Must

During all phases of our defensive work we elaborate frequently on the importance of gang tackling. We like to see six or seven of our players in on every tackle. Such tactics are not only demoralizing to ball carriers and wear them down physically, but represent sound football. It is difficult for the ball carrier to break loose and score when half a dozen men are fighting to get a piece of him.

We want the first tackler to get a good shot at the ball carrier, making certain he does not miss him. We want the other defenders to "tackle the ball," and make the ball carrier fumble it so we can get possession of the football. We are trying to get possession of the football any way we can. Frankly, we want the first man to the ball carrier merely to hold him up, and not let him get away, so we can unload on him. You can punish a ball carrier when one man has him "dangling," and the others gang tackle him hard. I am not implying we want our boys to pile on and play dirty football merely to get a ball carrier out of the game. First, we do not teach this type of football as it is a violation of the rules and spirit of the game. Second, piling on brings a 15-yard penalty. We cannot win when we get penalized in clutch situations.

OUR DEFENSIVE NUMBERING SYSTEM
AND TERMINOLOGY

After coaching for a number of years, and always trying to find something that would make football easier to understand for the average player, I came upon a system of defensive numbering that has proven very valuable to me since then. In the past I have used many different defenses. I always employed the technique of giving each defense a name. Most of the time the name had little in common with the defense, and this confused, rather than helped, the players. After discussing the possibility of the numbering system with my own and other college and high school coaches, while at Texas A&M, I finally came across a feasible plan for numbering defensive alignments. I must give credit to O. A. "Bum" Phillips, head coach of the New Orleans Saints, for working out the system. Bum was a high school coach at the time, and later worked on my staff at Texas A&M in 1958.

In the numbering of our defense now, we give a number to each offensive man as well as to the gaps between the offensive linemen. Figure 1 is an example of our defensive numbering system.

Figure 1

Accompanying each number is a particular "technique," which will be explained shortly. If a defensive player lines up in a 2 position, he will play what we call a "2 technique"; a 3 position plays a "3 technique," etc. Therefore, from end to end of the offensive line we can line up our defensive men and each position has a particular technique.

Who calls the defense? How is it called and what does it mean? Who is included in the call? Each linebacker calls the defense for his particular side of the line. He controls his guard, tackle and himself, but he does not control the end on his side of the line. The latter is controlled by the defensive signal caller in the secondary who gives a call for the 4-or 5- spoke defensive alignment.

Each linebacker calls two numbers. The first number tells his guard where to line up and his accompanying defensive technique. The second number gives the same information to the defensive tackle.

As an example, if the linebacker calls, "26," the guard will play a 2 technique and the tackle a 6 technique. If the caller said, "59," the guard would play a 5 technique and the tackle a 9 technique. When the linebacker tells the guard and tackle which techniques to play through his oral call, then he lines up in a position to cover the remaining gaps. As an example, Figure 2 illustrates a 26 call, and the linebacker must take a position between his guard and tackle so he can fill the gap(s) not covered by the other front defenders. You can see by this example the linebacker is in a position to help out over the offensive tackle position, and also on a wide play to his side of the line.

Figure 2

Figure 3 illustrates the position of the defensive right guard, tackle and linebacker when the call is 59. The linebacker is now in a position to help out on a play that is in the middle of the line.

Figure 3

One point I failed to mention, if we are playing a 4-spoke defense, which will be explained and illustrated shortly, we assign one defender to play "head-on" the offensive center, and he does not figure in any of the calls. He lines up the same every time, as is illustrated in Figure 4.

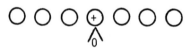

Figure 4

When we play a 5-spoke defense, which will also be explained shortly, the two linebackers assign one player to the area inside the offensive guards. As an example, if we are playing a 5-spoke defense and the call on the right side is 59, the call on the left side must be a one as the first digit, such as, 17, 16, 15. Figure 5 illustrates a 59 call on the right, and a 17 call on the left, with one man playing a 1 technique in order to keep from having a large gap between the two guards.

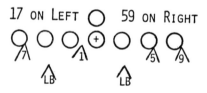

Figure 5

You can quickly observe that by having our players learn only a few numbers and their accompanying techniques, we can line up in numerous defensive alignments merely by calling two numbers. Figures 6 and 7 are examples of 59 and 39 defensive calls, which are 4-spoke defenses with a man in a 0 technique, and are commonly referred to as the Oklahoma and Eagle defenses, respectively.

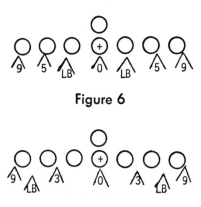

Figure 6

Figure 7

Figure 8 illustrates a 25 call, with a 0 technique, and is a 9-man front defensive alignment.

Figures 9-11 are 5-spoke defenses representing 26, 37, and 13 calls, which are commonly referred to as a wide tackle 6, a split 6, and a gap 8 alignment, respectively.

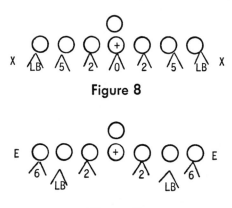

Figure 8

Figure 9

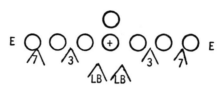

Figure 10

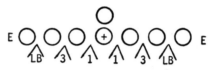

Figure 11

These defenses, Figures 6-11, have the same call to each side. Each side is actually independent of the other as far as the calls are concerned. To eliminate any confusion, merely designate which side (left) is to call first, and the other linebacker (right) can adjust on his call accordingly so there is not a large gap in the middle of the defensive line. The linebackers must be especially aware of this if we are employing a 5-spoke defensive alignment.

The signal caller should never call a defense involving two successive numbers, such as 2-3, 7-6, as this will leave too much territory for him to try to cover (see Figure 1). The caller is always responsible for having a man in or capable of covering, every gap.

It is very simple for the defensive signal caller to change the guard and tackle assignments even after he has given them a position to line up in and its accompanying technique. The caller merely adds a zero (0) or a one (1) to the end of the number he has called. As an example, if he gives the call 37 and he wants the players in the 3 technique to charge one-half a man toward the inside, he will say, "30." If he wants this defender to charge one-half a man to the outside, he would say, "31." This second call is given to only one player at a time, but he can change both of their techniques by saying, "31-71," or "30-70," etc.

Advantages of a Defensive Numbering System

Our present method is the simplest one I know of for getting players into various defenses quickly with a minimum amount of talking. We feel it eliminates much confusion. We have found the players take a great deal of pride in learning only a few techniques, which they are able to execute well. We know it makes our job easier as coaches, and we can do a better job of coaching the players. As a coaching point, when a coach talks to a tackle, as an example, he talks in terms of a particular technique (6, 7, etc.), and the player understands him immediately. When the coaches are discussing plays, or in a staff meeting, we identify the particular technique immediately, and everyone understands each other. We have also found the method useful when making out the practice schedule as I merely specify, "Tackle coach work on 6 technique," etc.

Employing a defensive numbering system requires the defensive signal callers to be alert. They do not merely call several numbers. They must be aware of the tactical situation at all times, and call a sound defense according to a tactical and strategical planning. As an illustration, a good short yardage call would be 13, and sound passing situation calls would be 36, 37, 39, 59 (see Figures 1, 3, 6, 7, 10, 11). I spend at least several minutes every day with my defensive signal callers. It is the linebackers' responsibility to see that we line up in a sound alignment every time.

PLAYING OUR DEFENSIVE TECHNIQUES

As illustrated in Figure 1, and mentioned earlier, our techniques and defensive positions are numbered from 0-9 on both sides of the defensive line, numbering from inside-out (with certain exceptions noted, Figure 1). I now wish to explain in detail each particular technique, although there is only a slight difference between several of them. As an example, when playing the 2 technique, a defender lines up head on the offensive guard, and when playing a 4 technique he is head up on the offensive tackle. Consequently these techniques are similar.

The 0 Technique

As illustrated in Figure 12, the defender lines up head on the offensive center. Depending upon the situation, the distance he lines up off the football will vary. On a short yardage situation, he will line up close to the center's head. On a long yardage situation,

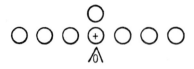

Figure 12

normally he will be about one yard off the ball. He will use either a three- or a four-point stance, with one foot staggered. His technique is to play the center's head with a quick hand shiver on the snap of the ball. When he makes contact with the center, he brings his back foot up so his feet are even with each other. If the quarterback goes straight back to pass, the 0 technique man is responsible for the draw play, and then he rushes the passer. If it is a run instead of a pass play, he will keep the center away from his blocking surface, not permitting himself to be tied up in the middle of the line, and he will pursue the ball, taking his proper angle depending on the type of running play.

When the 0 technique man is double-teamed, he is taught to hold his ground and not to spin out because a linebacker will be filling the area where the offensive guard lined up. He does not want the center to be able to cut him off.

The 1 Technique

The main job of the player(s) employing the 1 technique is to control the offensive splits, forcing the guards to keep their splits to a minimum, as illustrated in Figure 13. He is also responsible for keeping the center off the defensive linebacker. If both guards are playing in this technique, as illustrated in Figure 13, only one will "slam" the center, and the other will take a long step toward his guard, playing him from inside-out. He must always be aware of the trap coming from the inside, however. If the play is a back-up pass, he is responsible for the draw first, and rushing the passer second. If it is a running play, he will slam the center or guard and then pursue the football.

When he "feels" a trap, he must not cross the line of scrimmage, but he should "attack" the trapper and not let the trapper move him out. In order to play this technique properly, you should never let the center cut you off when a play is coming your way.

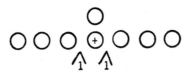

Figure 13

The 2 Technique

The 2 technique is similar to the 0 technique, and is illustrated in Figure 14. One difference is the guard is head on the offensive guard, instead of on the offensive center. The distance he lines up off the ball in a staggered stance will be determined by the tactical situation. On the snap of the ball he plays the guard with a hand shiver, and immediately locates the football. If it is a back-up pass and there is no man in a 0 or 1 technique, he will look for the draw play first, and then rush the passer. If it is a running play, he will look first toward the inside for a trap, and then pursue the football. Do not let the center cut you off on a running play your way. If you are playing against a guard that pulls, you should develop a looping technique that will allow you to "catch" any play where he pulls. Do not let the tackle block back on you.

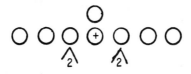

Figure 14

The 3 Technique

The 3 technique is similar to the 1 technique, and is illustrated in Figure 15. The 3 man is responsible for keeping the offensive tackle's split cut down, and on occasion, to keep the offensive guard or tackle from blocking the defensive linebacker. He, too, lines up with the feet slightly staggered, and about one foot off the ball. Depending upon the defense, when the ball is snapped, he will play either the guard or tackle with a quick flipper or shiver, preferably with the hands. He is to watch for the trap at all times. If the play is a straight drop-back pass, he will rush the passer from the inside. If it is a running play, he will pursue the football. The 3 technique man should never let the guard "slip" him and keep him out of a wide play his way.

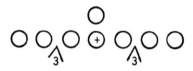

Figure 15

The 4 Technique

The 4 technique man lines up head on the offensive tackle and about one to one and one-half feet off the ball, and is illustrated in Figure 16. He will have his feet slightly staggered, and on the snap of the ball he is to play the offensive tackle with a quick hand or forearm flipper. If it is a running play toward him, he must whip the offensive tackle, be ready to stop the hand-off, and help out on the off-tackle play. If it is a straight-back pass, he will rush the passer from the inside. If the play goes away or to the far side, he will control the offensive tackle and pursue the football. On his angle of pursuit, he should never go around the offensive tackle, but pursue the football going through the tackle's head.

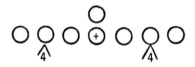

Figure 16

The 5 Technique

The 5 technique man lines up on the outside eye of the offensive tackle, as illustrated in Figure 17, with the feet staggered (outside foot back in most cases). On the snap of the ball, he employs a forearm flip charge into the tackle. As he makes contact, his back foot is brought up even with his front foot. He has 75 percent off-tackle responsibility, and he should never be blocked in by only one man. If it is a straight-back pass, he should rush the passer from inside-out. If the play comes toward him, he should whip the tackle and make the play. He must be certain to keep the offensive blocker in front of him at all times as the 5 man will be eliminated from the play very easily if he tries to go around his blocker. If the play goes away from him, he must pursue the football. He is instructed not to cross the offensive line of scrimmage when employing a 5 technique. If the 5 technique is double-teamed, he tries to hold his ground and not spin out immediately. He does not want to be driven back and force his linebacker to go around him. He should never let the tackle block him in and if the tackle blocks down, he should look for the end to try to block him in. If the tackle goes to his outside across his face, he should anticipate an influence play and be ready to play off a trap from his inside.

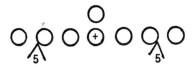

Figure 17

The 6 Technique

The 6 technique player lines up head on the offensive end, as illustrated in Figure 18. If the end splits too far, the 6 man is to "shoot the gap." He is primarily responsible for keeping the offensive end from releasing quickly on passes, and he must keep the end from blocking the linebacker. He is responsible for the off-tackle play. Consequently, he must not be blocked in or out. The game situation will determine how far he lines up off the ball, but it will usually vary from one to three yards. If the play is a straight-back pass, he is responsible for rushing the passer from the outside-in. If the passer runs out of the pocket, the 6 man must not permit him to get to the outside. He must either tackle the passer or force him to throw the football. If the play comes toward the 6 man, he whips the end with a flip or shiver charge, and helps out both inside and outside. He never crosses the line of scrimmage unless it is a back-up pass. If it is an option play toward him, he must make the quarterback pitch the ball or he must tackle the quarterback. If the flow goes away from him, he trails the play. He should be as deep as the deepest man in the offensive backfield so he can contain the reverse play back to his side, not permitting the ball carrier to get outside of him.

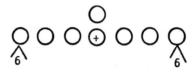

Figure 18

The 7 Technique

The 7 technique player lines up splitting the inside foot of the offensive end, as illustrated in Figure 19. He is responsible for forcing the end to reduce his offensive split. We want him to line up with his outside foot staggered, and he must never be blocked out by the offensive end. He has 75 percent inside responsibility and 25 percent outside responsibility. When the ball is snapped, he uses a hand or forearm flipper charge on the offensive end and brings his back foot up even with his front foot. His main responsibility is to whip the offensive end, and to close the off-tackle play. If the play is a straight drop-back pass, he is the outside rusher and he must not permit the quarterback to get outside of him. If the play goes away from him, he is to trail the ball carrier. He plays just like the trail or chase man on the 6 technique. He should be as deep as the deepest offensive backfield man so he can contain any reverse play coming back to his side of the line. He should not let such a play get outside of his position. If the offensive end releases to his outside real fast, he should expect a block from the fullback or a trap from the guard. In both cases, he should not work up field or to the outside. If an option should come your way and the end releases outside, make the quarterback pitch the ball.

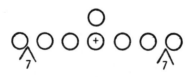

Figure 19

The 8 Technique

When we speak of a man playing an 8 technique, as illustrated in Figure 20, we are speaking of a "true end," or a defensive end who lines up outside of the offensive end. The 8 man will be from one and one-half to three yards outside of the offensive end's normal position, with his inside foot forward, and his shoulders parallel with the line of scrimmage. If it is a straight-back pass, the defensive end, without taking his eyes off the passer, will turn to his outside, and using a crossover step will sprint to his outside trying to get width and depth to play the ball to his side. His depth should be 8-10 yards deep, similar to a linebacker's position covering the flat. He stops running when the quarterback stops to set up. When the ball is thrown, he sprints for the ball.

If the play comes toward the 8 man, we want him to cross the line of scrimmage about two yards, getting set with his inside foot forward, shoulders parallel with the line of scrimmage, and playing the outside blocker. He is the outside contain man, and he must not permit the ball to get outside of him. He never makes the quarterback pitch on option plays. If it is a running pass toward him, he is the outside contain and rush man. If the flow goes away from him, he must make sure it is not a reverse play back to his side before he takes his proper angle of pursuit, which is through the area where the defensive safety man lined up originally.

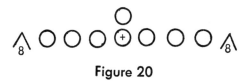

Figure 20

The 9 Technique

Figure 21 illustrates where the defensive men line up when playing a 9 technique, splitting the outside foot of the offensive end. He should line up 14 inches off the line of scrimmage, with most of his weight on the outside foot which is back. When the ball is snapped, the 9 technique man will take a short step with his inside foot toward the offensive end, and at the same time he will deliver a hand or forearm shiver to the head of the offensive end. If the offensive end blocks in and the play comes toward him, the 9 man immediately looks for the near halfback or the trapper expecting to be blocked by either offensive man.

If a running play comes toward him and the quarterback is going to option the football, he must make the quarterback pitch the ball. If the quarterback is faking the ball to the fullback, the 9 man must "search" the fullback for the ball first. The 9 technique man never crosses the line of scrimmage. If the offensive play is a straight-back pass, the 9 man delivers a blow to the end, and drops back two or three yards looking for the screen or short pass. He is in a position to come up and make the tackle if the quarterback gets outside of your outside rusher and the quarterback decides to run with the football. If the flow goes away, he is the trail man and has the same responsibilities as the 6 and 7 technique men, which I explained previously. The most important coaching point is that the man playing the 9 technique must deliver a good blow to the offensive end on every play. The 9 technique can never be "hooked" in by the end and at the same time, makes it hard for him to block down on your 5 technique.

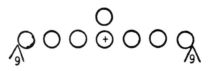

Figure 21

OUR DEFENSIVE STANCE

We are not too particular about the stance our defensive players employ, but on the other hand we are not so indifferent that we ignore how they line up defensively. We want them to be comfortable, but at the same time the linemen must be in a position to uncoil and make good contact, and be in a good position so they can move quickly. We never permit a man to take a stance in which he gets too extended and loses most of his hitting power. There are a few basic techniques we insist our defensive players use. These techniques vary to some extent from position to position. The defensive stance for linemen, linebackers and the secondary is as follows:

Guards—The defensive stance our guards take is very similar to the stance we use offensively. We like them to be in a four-point stance with their feet even and spread about three inches wider than their shoulders. The weight must be slightly forward, and their tail slightly higher than their shoulders. Their back is straight, and their shoulders are square. Their hands are slightly outside of their feet, elbows relaxed, with thumbs turned in and forward of the shoulders slightly.

Tackles—The defensive stance our tackles take is very similar to the stance we use offensively. We want our tackles to use a four-point stance, having their inside foot staggered back slightly. Their feet should be a little wider than their shoulders. The weight must be forward slightly. and the tail should be slightly higher than the head. Just like the guards' stance, we want their back straight and their shoulders square. Their neck must be relaxed, but their eyes must be focused on the man opposite or on the ball. The hands are slightly outside of the feet, elbows relaxed, and the thumbs turned in and forward of the shoulders slightly.

Ends—The defensive ends line up with their inside foot forward and perpendicular to the line of scrimmage. We want our ends standing up in a good football position. The knees are slightly bent, and their body bent forward slightly at the waist. They must have their eyes on the quarterback, but still be able to see the offensive halfback and end closest to them on their side. When the action starts toward an end, we want him to come across the line and make contact with the outside blocker. The shoulders should remain parallel with the line of scrimmage upon contact with an offensive back.

Linebackers—We want our linebackers to be standing with their feet even and parallel with each other. They should be in a good football position—tail down, back straight, slightly bent at the waist, weight on the balls of the feet, knees bent, and coiled to the extent that when a guard or tackle fires out on the linebacker the defensive man can whip him. Our linebacker takes a step forward with the inside foot toward the blocker who is firing out at him. We want him to drop his tail and hit on the rise when making contact. He then brings his back foot up even with his forward foot so that he will be in a position to move laterally.

Rover—Our defensive rover lines up in his regular position which is three yards outside of the offensive end in a 3-deep defense, and on the inside shoulder of the offensive end in a 4-spoke defense. We want our rovers to have their outside foot forward with the inside foot back. The outside foot is about 14 inches in front of the front foot, and pointing out at a 45 degree angle. The rover's knees should be flexed slightly, and he must be in a good football position. His arms should be in a cocked position. He must face the quarterback. His first step is slightly backward.

Corner man—The corner man lines up in his regular position about four yards wide and two and one-half yards deep, with his feet parallel and even about 18 inches apart, pointing directly toward the offensive quarterback. He should be in a good football position, weight on the balls of the feet, arms cocked, etc. He should not rest his hands on his knees. From a good football position he can rotate quickly and properly, he can come forward and meet the play if it comes toward him.

Safety—The safety man lines up a little deeper than the other backs. He should face slightly toward the wide side of the field or the strong side of the offensive backfield. He has his outside foot back, and is permitted to stand a little straighter than the other deep backs. He, too, is in a good football position watching the quarterback. His first step is backward and outward, and he must be able to cover a pass from sideline to sideline.

OUR SURPRISE DEFENSE

We never send our players into a football game without trying to prepare them for every conceivable situation that might arise during the contest. We must try to anticipate every situation, and counteract with a sound defense. A situation might be very unusual, and we cannot actually defense it properly until the coach in the press box tells us exactly what the opposition is doing. Then we can work out the proper defense on the sideline and send it in. In the meantime, the players must have something they can counteract with immediately or the opposition is likely to score with its surprise offense. Consequently our signal caller will yell, "Surprise Defense," when he sees an unusual offensive formation, and the players will react accordingly. Our rules for covering a spread or unusual offensive alignment are as follows:

1. If one man flanks, our halfback will cover him.
2. If two go out, our halfback and end will move out and cover them.
3. If three men go out, our halfback, tackle and end move out and cover them.
4. If four offensive men go out, we put out the halfback, end and tackle, and our linebacker goes out half-way. The alignment for the linebacker would be a yard deeper and a yard wider than he usually lines up.
5. If five men go out on the offensive team, we put out our halfback, end, tackle, linebacker half-way, and the defensive guard. If they put more than five men out, we do not change our alignment.
6. If there is any doubt about how to meet strength with strength, we start with the outside man and put a defender on every other offensive man.
7. The safety man will always play in the middle of the field or in the middle of the eligible receivers.
8. A defensive end must never be flanked by one offensive man unless he can beat the flanker through the gap and into the offensive backfield.
9. A tackle should never be flanked by two offensive men unless he can beat the nearest opponent.
10. The initial charge of the players who are left on defense is to the outside, unless there is a concentration of offensive backs. Should the latter be the case, then the defensive charge will be normal.
11. The greater the offensive team splits its line, the farther off the line of scrimmage the defenders must play.

Figures 22-23 illustrate two examples of spread formations, and the application of our surprise defense coverage rules.

The first offensive man who flanks to our right (Figure 22), will be covered by our defensive right halfback. The second to our right will be covered by our right end. The first man flanked to our left will be covered by our offensive left halfback; the second man out, by our left end; the third flanker, by our left tackle; the fourth flanker will be covered by our left linebacker, who will move out half-way. The fifth man flanked to our left will be covered by our

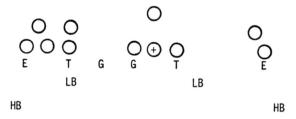

Figure 22

left guard. The remaining players will meet strength with strength. Our right guard will play on the outside shoulder of the offensive right guard, and the defensive right tackle will play on the outside shoulder of the offensive left guard, as illustrated in Figure 22.

We instruct our defensive players to force the offensive players to come to them. We do not want our men off the line of scrimmage to penetrate, leaving gaps in the defense. We want our men to be in a good football position so they can pursue the ball quickly.

Figure 23 illustrates another example of the application of our surprise defense rules in covering a spread offense.

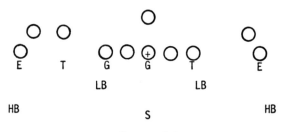

Figure 23

OUR VICTORY DEFENSE

I think it is very important for a team to be able to go into a "Victory Defense" when the occasion warrants its use; for example, when you have a slim lead with little time remaining before the termination of the first half or the game. We will go into a 3-man line if we have the game won and our opponents are not close to our goal line. Under such circumstances we can afford to permit the opposition to get a first down or two, but we cannot afford to let them complete the long pass or the long run for a touchdown. We believe our victory defense is sound, and we are playing sound defensive football when we employ it. Figure 24 illustrates the victory defense we used eight times in one year, and we intercepted our opposition's intended forward pass on seven of the eight occasions.

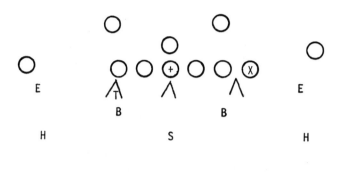

Figure 24

The individual and team duties and responsibilities when we employ our Victory Defense are as follows:

Middle Lineman—Sole responsibility is to look for the screen pass and/or for the draw play.

Ends and Tackles—Line up on the outside shoulder of the tackles. If the offensive end(s) split, we will adjust on them with our three deep backs. We want our defensive ends to shove the offensive ends to the inside, holding them up if possible, and then look to the inside for a trap block or for a screen pass. Should neither of these occur, the ends are to contain the passer, not permitting the ball to get outside either of their respective positions. They should play loose and proceed with caution, rather than rushing into the offensive backfield.

The defensive tackles should play back off the line of scrimmage with their feet even and parallel. Each tackle must keep his man in front of him, not permitting the offensive tackles to block them in or out. When a pass develops, the tackles must rush the passer, making certain to stay in front of the football.

Linebackers—Line up about six yards deep and at a spot opposite where the defensive end ordinarily would line up. By lining wide, we hope to funnel the offense toward the middle of our formation. By this I mean we want them to direct their attack toward the inside and we don't want them to turn the corner, to get outside or to kill the clock by running out-of-bounds.

Halfbacks and Safety—We want our halfbacks to be at least 12 yards deep and well outside the offensive formation. We want our safety man at least 12 yards deep and in the middle of our defensive alignment. The three backs will play their regular defense.

Best Defensive Player—The next step in setting up our Victory Defense is to station our best defensive football player 10 yards behind the middle safety man. His sole responsibility is to keep the offensive team from scoring. He must always stay between the ball and the goal line. We do not want him to come forward and break up a pass. Nor do we want him coming up to make the tackle. We want him to fight off blockers and make certain the ball carrier does not score should our defense break down and the opposition move downfield toward the goal line with a long run or a completed pass. When the ball is thrown, we want every man on the team to go for the ball except our deepest man, our best defensive football player. He remains 10 yards behind the ball at all times in case there is a tip and the opponent might catch it and score. His sole responsibility is to keep the opposition from scoring when we are using our Victory Defense.

OUR GOAL LINE DEFENSE

Our goal line defense is very simple, and I am certain many other coaches use the same goal-line defense, as illustrated in Figure 25. Perhaps there are a number of goal line defenses that are better than ours, but we have faith and believe in our goal line defense, and I believe this is 50 percent of the battle. When we go into our goal line defense, we want our players to be so sold on what they are doing that they are not going to let the opposition score. Each man is going to take it upon himself to see that they do not score over his particular defensive area. Playing goal line defense is a terrific challenge. There is not much territory remaining, and the big questions are, "Who is going to come out on top?" and "Who will end up with the ball when the dust settles?" If we give our team a sound

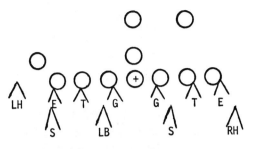

Figure 25

plan and teach it to them well, and they believe in it and in us, we will do all right.

Figure 25 illustrates our goal line defense, and the individual and team duties and responsibilities are as follows:

Ends—The defensive ends line up in a four-point stance as close to the line of scrimmage as they can get, just shading the outside eye of the offensive ends. On the snap of the ball, the defensive ends will charge low and hard through the tail of their offensive ends, trying to get approximately one yard deep into the offensive backfield. If the flow comes toward his side and the quarterback has the football, the defensive end tries to force the quarterback to pitch back to the off-halfback.

Tackles—The defensive tackles line up on the outside eye of the offensive tackles, and they aim for a spot one yard deep in the offensive backfield behind the inside foot of the offensive tackles. Each tackle is responsible for the hand-off play to his side, making the tackle or forcing the dive play to the inside so our middle linebacker can make the tackle.

Guards—The defensive guards get their spacing by lining up on each other, but theoretically they will line up on the inside eye of the offensive guards. They are responsible for sealing-off the middle of the line, and for keeping the offensive center from blocking the middle linebacker. They aim for a spot about one yard behind the offensive center's position. They must get to this spot using a low, hard submarine charge.

As illustrated in Figure 26, if our six linemen carry out their defensive assignments using a low, hard charge and get to their predetermined spots, we will form a wall.

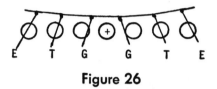

Figure 26

Linebackers or Safety (see Figure 25)—They are responsible for making any play that occurs between the offensive tackles. They should make the tackle on a hand-off, on a play up the middle, and help on the off-tackle play. On a back-up pass, they will drop off covering a short zone. If the play starts wide, the linebackers will pursue the football. They should be your best defensive football players. Figure 27 illustrates the defensive position and responsibilities of the linebackers in our goal line defense.

Figure 27

Halfbacks (see Figure 28)—The halfback is responsible for containing an end run to his side. If a running pass develops, he should be in the flat and alert to take the first receiver to his side. If the flow goes away, the halfback should check for someone coming back in a reverse of some kind, and if no one is coming, he should drop back and look for the tight end slipping across in case of a pass.

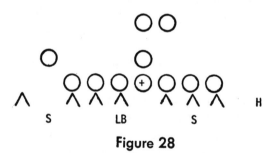

Figure 28

DEFENSE VERSUS OPTION

There are a number of good defenses versus a running team. I will go over several of the defenses we have used more frequently than others. Figure 29 illustrates our 59 call or the Oklahoma 5-4

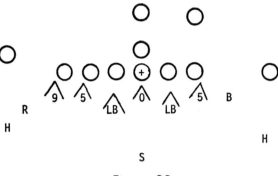

Figure 29

defense versus the T formation. The individual and team duties and responsibilities are as follows:

Ends—The defensive ends play a 9 technique, and on this particular defense, both ends' assignments and techniques will be identical. They will not penetrate beyond the line of scrimmage unless the flow is away. When the flow goes away, the off-side defensive end becomes the trail man.

Tackles—The defensive tackles play a 5 technique, which I discussed in detail earlier in the chapter. They will never cross the line except on a straight drop-back pass, and then both tackles will rush the passer. Otherwise, the tackles whip their respective opponents (tackles) and pursue the football.

Middle Guard—The middle guard plays a 0 technique, always alert for the screen pass or the draw play. On the snap of the ball, the middle guard should whip the offensive center and then go to the ball.

Linebackers—The inside linebackers will line up on the outside eye of their respective offensive guards, and "read" through them into the offensive backfield. If the offensive guards or tackles fire out, the linebackers whip them and go to the football. If the flow goes away, the off-side linebacker will check the counter play, and then pursue the football. On a drop-back pass, each linebacker will cover his short one-quarter pass zone or area.

The defensive secondary will play its regular 3-deep with a rover, and revolve on the plays after the offense shows what they are going to do (or from a pre-determined call, which will be explained shortly). The 4-spoke secondary will be discussed and illustrated in Chapter 5, "Pass Defense."

Figure 30 illustrates our 27 call or a wide tackle 6 defensive alignment versus the T formation.

We use a 6-2 alignment frequently because we can stunt easily or we can play it straight versus a long yardage situation, and we can jump from it into another defensive alignment without too much difficulty. The linebackers control their particular units, as I explained earlier. The individual and team duties and responsibilities are as follows:

Guards—The guards will play a tough 2 technique, then pursue the football. On a drop-back pass, they are responsible for the screen pass in the middle, the draw play, and rushing the passer.

Tackles—The tackles will play a tough 7 technique. They are responsible for the off-tackle play to their respective sides. If the play goes away, the tackle is the trail man. On back-up passes, the tackles rush the passer from the outside.

Ends—The defensive ends play an 8 technique, and they are the contain men if the flow comes their way. If the ball goes away, the off end drops back and pursues through the area where the safety lined up originally. On back-up passes, they will cover the short one-quarter pass areas or zones.

Linebackers—The linebackers line up on the inside eye of the offensive tackles, and play their regular positions. If the play comes toward them, the linebacker whips the blocker with a flipper and plays the ball carrier. When flow is away, he checks the counter play and then pursues the football. On pass plays, they will cover their short one-quarter pass zones.

Secondary—The defensive secondary will play their regular

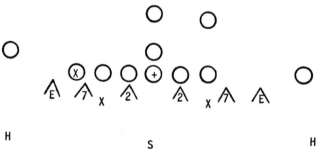

Figure 30

3-deep coverage, which will be explained in the next chapter. On wide running plays, the halfback must come up to the outside and turn the play back inside. The safety man comes up to the inside, playing inside-out, and off or far halfback revolves and becomes the last safety man.

Figures 31-34 illustrate several of our defensive stunts from a 6-2 alignment, which we have employed with success in the past.

In Figure 31, the linemen pinch sealing off the inside, and the linebackers cover outside.

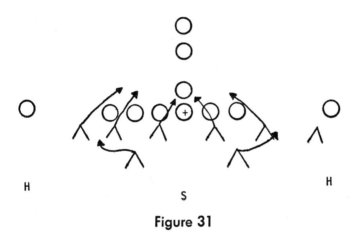

Figure 31

In Figure 32, the guards loop to the outside over the offensive tackles, and the linebackers fill inside the offensive guard splits.

Figure 32

Figure 33 illustrates a simple X-pattern between the defensive ends and tackles.

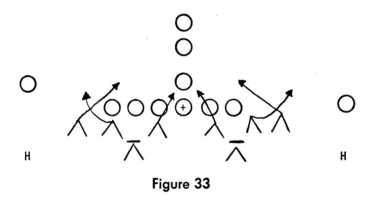

Figure 33

Figure 34 illustrates the tackles pinching, and the linebackers replacing them at the line of scrimmage over the offensive ends.

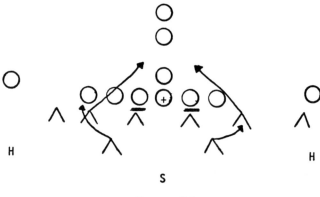

Figure 34

OUR DEFENSE VERSUS AN UNBALANCED LINE

We do not adjust a great deal to an unbalanced line, and our adjustments are relatively simple. We merely move our defensive line over one whole man, and then revolve the secondary toward the weak side, as illustrated in Figure 35.

When we do this, we carry out the same assignments, which I have explained earlier. The only difference is that our middle guard

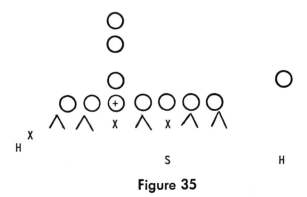

Figure 35

lines up on the offensive strong-side guard, instead of on the center. If we are playing a 3-deep defense, we would adjust with our linemen. Then we consider the strong guard as the middle of the offensive line (the center), and we play our regular defense.

ADJUSTMENTS VERSUS BACKS AND
ENDS FLANKED

When we have a defense called and the opposition comes out and lines up with a back or an end out, we can play it one of two ways. If it is a floater out or an end split, we will adjust slightly with our secondary, and we will drop the defensive end off the line a little. The remainder of the defensive linemen will play the defense that has been called. If a flanker is put out to one side or the other, we will revolve our 4-spoke secondary toward him and leave the linemen in their regular positions, or we will shift our line toward the flanker one whole man. These adjustments will be explained and illustrated more fully in Chapter 5, "Pass Defense."

In making our game plans, which will be discussed in Chapter 10, "Planning For a Game," we will always have a definite call that our signal caller will use in the situations discussed above relating to our adjustments versus backs and/or ends flanked out. As an example, we may tell our signal caller to shift our defense away from ends out and floaters, but shift toward flankers and an unbalanced line. These calls will depend upon the information we secure from scouting our opponents.

CHAPTER 5

Pass Defense:
Objectives and Tactics

TURNOVERS WILL GET YOU BEAT AND TURNOVERS WILL WIN FOR YOU—depending upon what you are playing. We think that to "intercept a pass" is very demoralizing to the opponent and it will get your defense out of a jam most of the time.

Basically, good pass defense is being in the proper position and playing the technique properly. At Alabama, we really stress technique and we try to eliminate the receiver more than "intercept" the ball. We think the interceptions will come if we are in the right spot doing the right thing.

We work on pass defense every day and when we have a player who can play man-to-man coverage, it makes things a lot easier. When the ball is in the air, we have two schools of thought: 1) the receiver cannot and must not catch it, and 2) the ball belongs to me and I take on the characteristics of a receiver and go to "catch" it rather than knock it down.

PASS DEFENSE OBJECTIVES

Pass defense is so vital that one simple defensive mistake can cost your team a football game. In order to have a good football team, the play in the defensive secondary must be sound.

The primary objective of pass defense is to keep the opponent from scoring, and second, to get the football. We stress these points all the time. On every play, we want each player trying to get possession of the football for our team.

Pass defense consists of the following phases:

1. Rushing the passer.
2. Holding up the receivers.
3. Covering the areas or zones.
4. Covering the receiver man-to-man.

We have found it difficult to do a good job on all four of these phases at the same time.

Rushing the Passer

Rushing the passer is the best way to play pass defense, especially with an 8- or 9-man line. Overloading one side of the line is a sound tactic, too, because you have more men rushing than the offense has blocking, and the quarterback must get rid of the ball quickly. If the quarterback has sufficient time to spot his receivers, then throw to one of them when he breaks to get open, it is difficult for the defense to cover the pass properly.

The men rushing the passer must have their hands up high, forcing the passer to release the ball higher than he does normally. Such tactics keep the passer from throwing the fast, straight, bullet-like pass, which is the hardest for the defenders to break up. Second, the rushers with their hands high cause the pass to remain in the air longer because of its upward trajectory as it is released. Consequently, this gives the defensive secondary time to release from their areas and sprint to the spot where the ball is descending.

The man who has the outside rush, and whose responsibility it is to contain, must get his hands high. He should not leap off the ground in an effort to tackle the passer, as he must be in a position to contain him in the event the passer tries to get out of the pocket and/or runs with the football.

When we are rushing the passer, we want our players to know they must not permit the passer to throw the football. In a definite passing situation when we decide to overload a zone and rush more men than the opposition has blockers, we acknowledge the fact we are sacrificing coverage in our secondary. Therefore, we must put on a strong rush, and we cannot permit the ball to be thrown on timing.

Figure 36 illustrates an overload on the right side of the offensive line. Analyzing the illustration and assuming it is a passing situation when we overload, if the opposition does throw a drop-back pass, we are in good shape because we have more rushers than they have blockers. If the opposition runs to their right, which would be our left, again we are sound defensively because they are running into our strength. In other words, we are 66-2/3 percent correct before the play even starts. If the opposition goes to their left (our right), we are not strong, but by our right side's hitting and sliding to the outside, as illustrated in Figure 36, we will not be hurt.

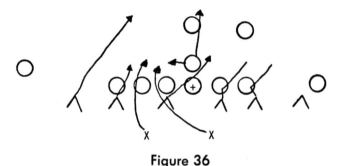

Figure 36

There are many ways of rushing a passer, but we do not expect to do a really good job of rushing unless we out-number the blockers. Then, when we have a pass rush called, our players know they cannot permit the passer to throw the ball on timing, as I cited previously.

Holding Up Receivers

We work on detaining the receivers at the line of scrimmage, but we probably do not devote enough time to this phase of pass defense. The purpose of this defensive tactic is to give your linebackers time to get to their defensive areas before the receivers get to them. It also gives your defensive halfbacks time to get their width and depth and get set up in their respective pass coverage zones. We hold up receivers several different ways as illustrated in Figures 37-39.

Figure 37 illustrates the tackle playing head up on the offensive end in order to detain him.

Figure 37

Figure 38 illustrates the defensive end and linebacker pinching off the offensive end, making it difficult for him to release for a pass.

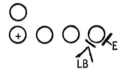

Figure 38

Figure 39 illustrates a third method of holding up an eligible receiver, merely by placing the linebacker in front of the offensive end so he can "whack" him as he releases from the line of scrimmage.

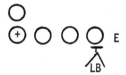

Figure 39

Covering the Areas

We cover the areas on pass defense, not the eligible receivers. We want our players to be in the middle of their areas in a good football position, and as soon as the ball leaves the passer's hand, we want our players to forget about everything else except intercepting the pass. We want our defenders to play through the receiver for the ball. They should never go around the receiver, unless it is a short pass. They should go for the ball at the highest point they can reach, and never catch the ball low if they could have intercepted the pass at a greater height. Our logic is that if a defender is waiting for the ball to come down so he can handle it at his chest or waist, the intended receiver has time to come in front of our defender and catch the pass for a completion. Whereas if our defender will go back when the ball is thrown, plant, and come toward the opponent's goal line intercepting the ball with arms and fingers extended upward, the intended receiver can't possibly take the ball away from him. This, of course, would depend upon the type of pass that was thrown.

MAN-TO-MAN PASS DEFENSE

There are times when we need to play man-to-man. We need to play it when we have a blitz called, or when we are playing against someone who has a strong running attack and will split out only one man and we want to cover that one person man-to-man. There are several basic steps that must be followed if this technique is to be played correctly, which are:

Alignment—It is important that you do not give your intentions away by your alignment. Use the same one that you use when playing a zone coverage.

Key—See something?—look for the flow of the backs, pulling lineman, action of the quarterback. What were your key calls for but to read something?

Backpedal—After the original key to confirm that you will be playing man-to-man on this play, go into a backpedal and gain the position that you want. The rule of thumb is—when the receiver is about 7 yards downfield, the defender should be about 2 yards off him and a yard inside or outside depending on the technique if it is inside or outside. Stay in the backpedal as long as you can and still feel you can cover the receiver deep. At any point you think the receiver will run by you, come out of the backpedal and run. You are backpedaling to gain a position and trying to maintain this position.

Concentration—This is the most important step in man-to-man coverage—CONCENTRATION. Do not let anything distract you from total concentration on the receiver. Never look at the quarterback until you are running stride-for-stride with the receiver. It takes a lot of self-discipline not to "peep" at the quarterback, but remember—the defender is not trying to intercept the ball when playing this technique. He is trying to keep the receiver from catching it.

Stride—After total concentration has been given to the receiver and you are in the proper relationship to him as he goes into his final break, you should be running with him stride-for-stride and only now will you look for the ball.

To review these steps, line up properly (alignment), key something (whatever you teach), backpedal for position (maintain it), concentrate (totally) and finally, as you are running stride-for-stride with the receiver, only then you can look for the ball.

OUR FIVE-SPOKE PASS DEFENSE

The 5-spoke or 3-deep, as it is commonly referred to at times, is a very sound defense in the secondary. Let me explain exactly what I mean by a 5-spoke defense. We compare the perimeter of our defensive secondary to one-half of a wheel, which may have 5 spokes or 4 spokes. The principles are basically the same, as you will see shortly. I shall discuss the 5-spoke defense first, however.

Figure 40 illustrates our 5-spoke defense. At the end of each of the imaginary spokes is a defender. The distance between the defenders depends on their individual ability. The spokes can be lengthened or shortened, but they should not be brought closer together or there will be a vulnerable area in the defensive secondary, as will be illustrated shortly. When the spokes of the wheel are lengthened, the players automatically become farther apart, depending upon the distance of the defenders from the football.

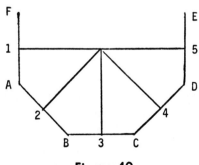

Figure 40

As illustrated in Figure 40, there are defensive men stationed at the ends of the spokes at points 1, 2, 3, 4, and 5. The defensive end located at 1 is able to cover the area from point F to A; the halfback at point 2 can cover the area from A to B; the safety at point 3 can cover the area from B to C; the halfback at point 4 covers C to D; and the end at point 5 can cover the area from D to E. If the length of the spokes is decreased, the area to be covered will not be as great. Conversely, the longer the spokes, the greater the area to be covered by the defensive secondary. If we stretch a wire from F to A to B to C to D to E, the area enclosed will represent the space in which we should be able to contain our opponents, as illustrated in Figure 40.

We want our players to assume that the half-wheel will revolve clockwise and counter-clockwise, but the defenders must always remain at their points at the end of the spokes, keeping the same relative distance from each other, in order for the defense to be sound. If the offensive team runs to their left, the wheel should revolve to our right, counter-clockwise, as illustrated in Figure 41. It would be just the opposite if the play were run to our left—revolve clockwise. If it were a running play up-the-middle, the spokes of the wheel would be shortened as the defensive men would converge on the ball carrier, keeping their same proportionate relationship to each other.

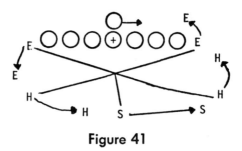

Figure 41

Figure 42 illustrates a vulnerable area in the defensive secondary as the result of the safety man's being out of position versus a back-up pass. His course should be straight back, covering the deep middle zone, so that he is approximately equidistant from his halfbacks. Should the error occur, as illustrated in Figure 42, our pass defense will not be sound.

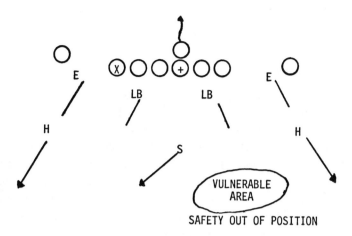

Figure 42

The length of the spokes will be determined by the distance of the defenders from the passer. As an example, if the passer goes back to throw off a drop-back action, the spokes would stretch proportionately. The defenders will have time to cover more distance if the passer is attempting to throw deep because the ball must remain in the air longer in order to reach its receiver. Conversely, if the passer attempts to throw a quick pass from only a yard or so off the line of scrimmage, the receivers will not have time to get deep; consequently, the length of the spokes will not be lengthened but will be shortened proportionately as the defenders converge on the ball as it is thrown.

Figure 43 illustrates the initial depth and width of the ends and the 3-deep secondary in the 5-spoke defensive alignment when the ball is in the middle of the field between the hash marks.

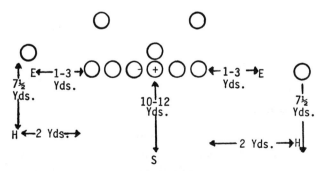

Figure 43

Keys for the 5-Spoke Defenders

Our 5-spoke defenders key as follows:

Ends—Our defensive ends look through the tail of the offensive ends and read the whole backfield, especially the back nearest to the defensive end and the uncovered lineman.

Halfbacks—They look through the offensive end to their side and read the whole backfield. It is very important that the halfbacks know at all times where the football is; consequently, they should watch the quarterback closely, as well as the flow of the backs.

Safety—The safety looks through the center, reading the quarterback and the whole offensive backfield. He, too, must know where the football is at all times, and he also keys the guards.

Linebackers—They line up on the tackle or guard, depending upon the particular front alignment we are employing at the time, and read the man in front of them. They should watch the entire backfield, too.

Figure 44 illustrates the positions and keys of the linebackers and the 5-spoke defenders.

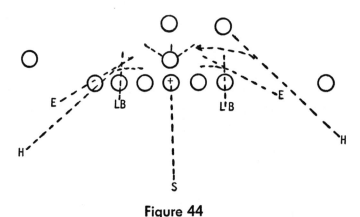

Figure 44

Dividing the Areas

We divide the areas in our defensive secondary into four short one-quarters and three deep one-thirds. The short one-quarters are covered by the ends and linebackers, and the halfbacks and safety cover the three deep thirds, as illustrated in Figure 45.

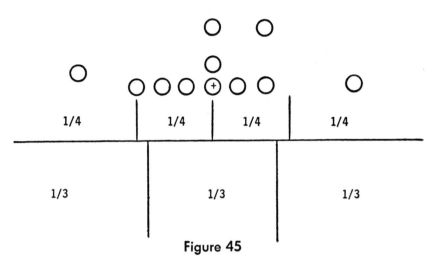

Figure 45

Our short one-quarter areas extend back 16 yards from the line of scrimmage because we are trying to force the passer to throw the football higher to his receivers behind our front line. We think that our linebackers can get back approximately 12-14 yards, but we always tell them we want them to cover 16 yards so they will hustle and work hard to get depth on their pass coverage. If we said only 12 yards, they might only get back to a depth of 10-12 yards, which would not be sufficiently deep to cover their zones.

If our inside linebackers drop back 16 yards and our corner linebackers drop to 8 yards, and if all four of these defenders are in a football position and ready to move, they should be able to touch any ball that is thrown in this area. There may be a ball thrown in front of our linebackers, but a completed pass in this area normally will not defeat us. We believe that if the passer goes back seven or eight yards, and our rushers can make him release the ball at a higher angle over their extended arms and fingers, it will be difficult for the passer to throw in front of the linebackers. Consequently, if they hustle and get to the depth I have indicated, they should be in a good position to intercept any ball thrown into their zone. We instruct our men in the short "fourths" to tip the ball when possible, providing they cannot intercept it, as one of our deep backs is likely to intercept a deflected pass. Incidentally, at times we will not have a defender in every "fourth" or only two of the "fourths" will be covered. At other times, we'll have an extra man in one of the "fourths."

After our linebackers get back to their positions, we want them to assume a relaxed position with the feet almost together, knees slightly bent, and ready to move in the direction indicated by their keys. We adopted this stance after making a study of baseball players relaxed and in an always ready-to-move position on the baseball field. We do not want our players to waste time and motion running in a circle getting to the football.

We can play only three men back in the deep zones. Therefore, we divide our deep zones into "thirds." A pass should never be completed in one of the deep zones if the line rushes hard forcing the passer to release the ball higher than usual, if the 3-deep men cover their zones properly, and if they see the ball leave the passer's hand and hustle to intercept it. Of course, teams do complete passes on us in these areas, but we do not believe it should ever happen. Each of the 3-deep men is a "guardian" of his particular area of the field, left, middle and right one-third.

The "thirds" will vary in size. As an example, if the football is over on the offensive team's left (our right) hash mark, the defensive right halfback's third would be smaller than the left halfback's one-third, as illustrated in Figure 46. The right halfback's one-third is smaller because of field position, and second because the ball has a relatively shorter distance to travel if thrown in this area of the field. Conversely, if the ball were thrown in the left halfback's area, the ball would be in the air longer on a deep pass and both defender and receiver would have farther to go to get to the ball. Therefore, the defensive left halfback's "third" would be larger and farther removed from the ball on the opposite hash mark.

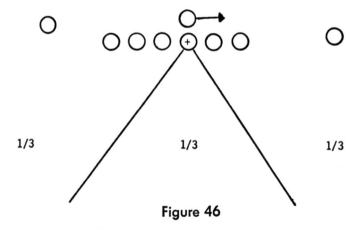

Figure 46

OUR PASS COVERAGE

We normally want a man in every area on our pass coverage, unless we decide for one reason or another not to cover one of the "fourths," as I indicated previously we sometimes do. The defender must intercept or knock down any and all passes thrown in his area. The defenders do not play man-to-man in their areas, but each man covers a zone. If he will play in the middle of his zone or area, when the ball is thrown he can go to it. If a defender plays a man instead of his zone, the decoy can take him out of his area, permitting another receiver to catch the ball. Then our defense is not sound. Therefore, we stress zone converage, and playing the ball unless we are in a man-to-man defense.

Coverage of Straight Drop-Back Pass

We consider a pass that is thrown from between the offensive tackle positions a straight drop-back pass, as shown in Figure 47.

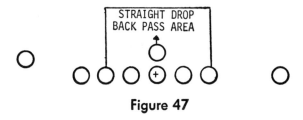

Figure 47

Figure 48 illustrates our coverage of the zones versus a straight drop-back pass. The defenders' duties and responsibilities are as follows:

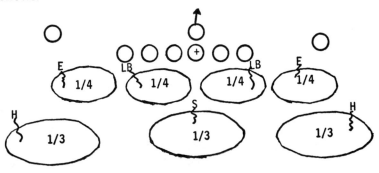

Figure 48

Defensive Right End—Turns to his outside, sprints back and out to a depth of 10 yards. He then sets up and faces the passer. He covers a short one-quarter zone. When the ball is thrown, he sprints for it.

Defensive Right Linebacker—Using a cross-over step, he turns to the outside and sprints back trying to get a depth of 12-14 yards. He must set up when the passer sets up. He keeps his distance with his other linebacker to the inside. When the ball is thrown, he sprints for it.

Defensive Right Halfback—His first step is backward and outward, and he continues to go back covering his deep one-third zone. He should not get closer than five yards to the sideline. When the ball is thrown, he breaks for it.

Defensive Safety—He should favor the wide side of the field when he retreats to cover his middle one-third zone. If no one is coming into his area, he should favor the side with two receivers out. When the ball is thrown, he breaks for it.

Defensive Left Halfback—His first step is backward and outward, and he continues to go back covering his deep one-third zone. He should never get closer than five yards to the sideline. When the ball is thrown, he breaks for it.

Defensive Left Linebacker—He turns to his outside and sprints back, using a crossover step, and tries to get a depth of 12-14 yards. However, he must set up when the passer stops and sets up. He keeps his distance with the linebacker to the inside. When the football is thrown, he sprints for it.

Defensive Left End—He turns to his outside and sprints backward and outward to a depth of 10 yards, and faces the passer. He covers a short one-quarter zone. When the football is thrown, he sprints for it.

Coverage of an Action Pass

Figure 49 illustrates our coverage versus an action pass. The defenders' duties and responsibilities are as follows:

Defensive Right End—He comes across the line of scrimmage and contains the play very fast. He must make the quarterback throw before the receiver has time to get too deep.

Defensive Right Linebacker—Plays the run first, then gets back to his area, but a little wider than normal.

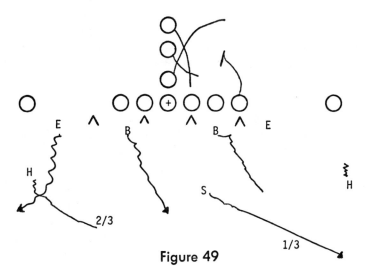

Figure 49

Defensive Right Halfback—His first step is slightly to the outside and back. His responsibility is the short one-quarter area. If he sees the wing running deep, he will try to slow him down by hitting him.

Defensive Safety—When he recognizes an action pass or a pass that gets outside of the tackle, he really takes off because his responsibility is the deep one-third to the side of the action.

Defensive Left Halfback—His first step will be to his inside and back because he will recognize the pass is going away from him and his responsibility is two-thirds of the field.

Defensive Left Linebacker—After playing for the run, he will turn to sprint for the area in front of the center about 18 yards deep. He must help the offensive halfback in this area.

Defensive Left End—After he sees the flow is going away from him, he turns to his inside and drops straight back, getting a lot of depth and taking anything to the outside that is up to 20 yards.

PASS DEFENSE BY POSITIONS

Defensive End (Flow toward a defensive end)—After lining up in his proper stance and position, when he sees the action coming toward him, he crosses the line of scrimmage approximately two yards deep in the offensive backfield. His inside foot should be forward, and his shoulders parallel to the line of scrimmage, as he plays off the outside blocker. He must contain the passer quickly. He cannot permit the passer to get outside of his position. On certain defenses, he will drop off and cover the short flat, especially when a back is flanked to his side of the field.

Defensive End (Versus drop-back pass)—After lining up in his proper stance and position, when he recognizes a drop-back pass, he turns to his outside and sprints, using a crossover step, to a spot 10 yards deep. He never takes his eyes off the passer. When the passer gets set to throw the ball, the defensive end must stop and set up, even if he has only gotten five yards deep. He must get into a good football position quickly, which is tail down, head up, back straight, weight on the balls of the feet, knees slightly bent and feet even. When the passer steps in one direction, as if to throw or fake the pass, we want the end to start in that direction, even if he "takes the fake." Should the latter occur and the passer not throw the football, then the end must bring himself under control quickly and sprint for the football when the passer releases it, regardless of where it is thrown.

Defensive End (Flow away from the defensive end)—After taking his proper stance and position and recognizing that the play is going away from him, he commences his angle of pursuit through the area where the defensive safety man lined up originally. When he sees a pass develop, he stops and still facing the passer and wide side, he tries to get back into a position to help out in the deep off one-third. He gets as deep as he can and puts his hands high. Consequently, the passer must throw the ball high to get it over him. Since the ball is thrown higher, it stays in the air longer and gives our defensive halfback who is covering that third of the field time to react and sprint for the football. When the ball is thrown, the end must sprint for it.

Defensive Linebackers (Versus straight drop-back pass)—If, after lining up in their proper positions and stance, they recognize the play as a straight drop-back pass, the linebackers will turn to their outside and by using a crossover step they will sprint back trying to get to a depth of 12-14 yards. They should never take their eyes off the passer. As soon as he gets set to throw, the linebackers should set up in a good football position regardless of their depth at the time. The linebackers must take the first passing fake of the quarterback or they will never be able to knock down the short passes. When the ball is thrown, they both must sprint to it.

Defensive Linebacker (Flow pass toward a linebacker)—After the linebacker has lined up in his proper stance and position and recognizes the flow is coming toward him, he must expect a running play first. The hole he must check will depend upon the defense that has been called. After he has checked for a run but sees a pass developing, he must turn to his outside and sprint for his short one-quarter area using a crossover step, or he will sprint to the flat on his side and cover this area. He, too, must get set when he sees the passer get set, and he takes the first fake. If the ball is not thrown, he regains his balance, position, etc. and sprints for the ball when it is thrown.

Defensive Linebacker (Flow away from the linebacker—From his proper stance and position, when he observes the flow going away from him, he steps in and checks the counter play and then starts his pursuit for the football. When he recognizes a pass developing, he will plant and try to get back to his short one-quarter area by using a crossover step. He will continue to go back to his one-quarter area still facing the direction of the flow. He is trying to get to a depth of 12-14 yards. However, he must come under control and maintain a good position when the quarterback gets set to pass. He then plays his regular pass defense. He must try to maintain his proper distance between his other linebacker as a short one-quarter area will be vulnerable if they move too close together. When the ball is thrown, he sprints for it.

Defensive Halfbacks (Versus straight drop back pass)—After the defensive halfbacks have lined up in their proper stance and positions and the ball is put into play, their first step is back and out. Each halfback starts toward his deep one-third zone as he sees the straight drop-back pass develop. Although they commence slowly, the longer the passer holds the ball, the faster and deeper they cover their one-third areas. The deep men do not take the passing fake, as the ends and linebackers must do. When the ball is put into the air in his area, the halfback must sprint to intercept the pass. It is very important that the halfbacks take the shortest and straightest line to the football once it leaves the passer's finger tips.

The defensive halfback will never get closer than five yards to the sideline when he is covering a deep one-third of the field. As he gets close to the sideline and the passer is still holding the football, the defensive halfback will bend away for the sideline but still remain in a position to see it.

If the ball is thrown deep over his head, the halfback is permitted to turn his back (whirl around) on the passer and go after the football. We feel he can cover more ground and get to the ball faster using the whirl-around method than if he plants, pivots, keeps his eye on the ball, and then goes after it. This is the only time we will permit a deep one-third defender to take his eyes off the football.

Defensive Halfback (Flow pass toward a defensive halfback)—After the halfback has lined up in his regular position and he recognizes an action pass or a running pass coming toward him, he starts back and out. His area of responsibility is the deep one-third to his side of the field. He must always be as deep as anyone in his area, and he must be in a position so that he can cover his whole zone. If the football comes into his zone, he is responsible for it. He must play the ball at the highest possible point he can reach it safely. He must not get closer than five yards to the sideline because this cuts down his ability to cover the entire one-third, his responsibility. When the ball is thrown, he must sprint for it. If his responsibility is to cover the short one-quarter area, he must be thinking to hit the wing and slow him down so his safety can get over to cover the deep one-third area.

Defensive Halfback (Flow pass away from the halfback)—After lining up in his proper position and stance and recognizing the flow is starting away from him on the snap of the football, his first step is back and out. He must get his width in case of a roll-out pass. On his third step he will plant, pivot to his inside, and get depth covering the one-third to his side of the field. Regardless of flow or action his pass responsibility is the deep one-third of the field that he lines up in. If his responsibility is the two-thirds area, then his first thought is to get depth and get into the middle of his two-thirds area. He must get help from the offside linebacker as well as the offside end.

Defensive Safety (Versus straight drop back pass)—After the safety has lined up in his proper position and stance and he sees the ball has been put into play, his first step is back and out, favoring the wide side of the field. He starts running slowly, but the deeper he goes, the faster he runs. He cannot permit a receiver to get behind him. He must be as deep as the deepest receiver anywhere on the football field. His responsibility is the deep middle one-third, and if the ball is thrown in his area, he must play the ball and not the receiver. We instruct the safety man to be deep enough so that he must come forward to play the football in the air instead of running backward to play it. If the ball is thrown in one of the deep one-third areas to his right or left, he does not sprint for the ball. Instead he sprints for a spot between the place where the ball will come down and the opposition's goal line. In case the opponent catches the ball, he will be in a position to tackle the receiver. If the ball is tipped into the air, the safety man should be in a position to catch the ball. He must remember that he is the safety and it is his duty to stop the opposition from scoring if they get past the other 10 defensive men.

Defensive Safety (Flow pass in any direction)—After the safety has lined up in his proper position and stance and sees the flow pass develop, his first step is back and out toward the flow. His area of responsibility is the deep middle one-third of the field, but he goes back facing or favoring the flow. He must get as deep as the deepest receiver and be in a position to cover the middle one-third, as well as be in a position to help out on deep passes from sideline to sideline. He must remember he is the safety, and he must prevent the touchdown regardless of where the ball is thrown. If his responsibility is to cover the deep one-third to the side of the action, he must really move in a hurry. He cannot depend upon the strong-side halfback to slow the wing down. He must line up in a position where he can get to the wing if the wing runs a streak and no one slows him down.

All Defenders When the Ball is Thrown—When the ball is thrown to any deep one-third area, the procedure is the same. Let's assume the play is a straight drop-back pass and it is thrown into our defensive right halfback's one-third zone area, as illustrated in Figure 50. If he is in the proper position, he will give an oral signal while the ball is still in the air. His signal tells the other defenders he is going to touch the football, and they should get set in the event it is tipped into the air. The safety will get between the halfback and the opposition's goal line. He should assume a good football position and be alert for the tipped football from his halfback. The defensive ends, linebackers and the other defensive halfback will be sprinting for the football. When they hear the right halfback's oral signal, they will stop about five yards away from him, get into a good football position, and watch for the tip. If our defender intercepts the football, his teammates will turn around quickly and block aggressively for him. The technique as I have described it is illustrated in Figure 50.

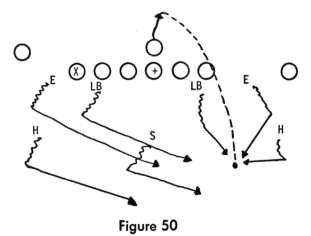

Figure 50

ADVANTAGES OF THE 5-SPOKE PASS DEFENSE

The advantages of the 5-spoke pass defense are as follows:

1. We always have a safety on alignment. This helps the cornerbacks.
2. The 3-deep men only have one position to learn on defense. The defensive right halfback is always the defensive right halfback, etc.
3. When the offense flanks backs and splits ends, it is easy to adjust our defensive backs. Instead of revolving, they simply loosen up or line up wider and still play their regular positions.
4. There is always a defender in each of the deep one-third areas without revolving into the area, unless we elect to revolve.
5. It is easier to cover the running pass because there is no point of indecision.
6. On a straight drop-back pass, there is a defender in every deep one-third area and one in every short one-quarter area.
7. We can get fast containment versus the action pass because ends line up in a wide position initially.
8. It is easy to teach because we delegate a definite area of responsibility on every occasion.

9. It is a very good defense against the long pass because of the deep centerfielder or safety man.
10. Keying is cut to a minimum because there is no revolving necessary in order to get a man in the deep safety position.

THE 4-SPOKE PASS DEFENSE

We use the 4-spoke more than we do the 5-spoke defense. There were times when this was just the opposite. It takes a better athlete to play the 4-spoke and because of movement, different formations, types of formations we see and the people available to play, we use the 4-spoke concept most of the time.

Advantages of the 4-Spoke Defense

The advantages of the 4-spoke defenses are as follows:

1. When playing a 9-man front, the extra man is always where you need him.
2. You can stunt a great deal in your secondary and give the passer problems.
3. It is a good defense against multiple sets.
4. Tremendous pursuit can be obtained from this formation because the linemen all play an outside technique.
5. You can pre-determine your rotation; consequently, you remove any indecision.
6. You use the same coverage with your goal line defense, merely tightening up the defense and the secondary.
7. You put quick pressure on the passer by using your 9-man front advantageously.
8. The defensive keys are definite.
9. It is easy to blitz from this pass defense.

The principle of the 5-spoke pass defense and the 4-spoke pass defense is basically the same with the exception that you have only four spokes or four men in the outer perimeter of your secondary. The spokes run from an imaginary center with a defender placed on the end of each spoke, as illustrated in Figure 51.

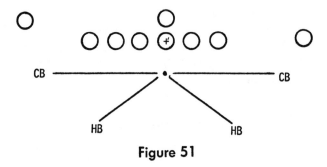

Figure 51

These spokes can all be lengthened or shortened, as we explained previously for the 5-spoke defense. They must move as a unit or team, however, or there will be vulnerable areas in the secondary. We run an imaginary line from defender to defender, considering the lines as a rubber band, as illustrated in Figure 52. The rubber band can stretch, but it should not break.

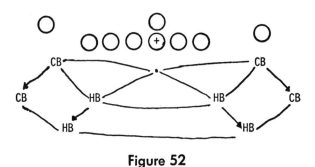

Figure 52

In Figure 52, the spokes have lengthened, the rubber band has stretched, and the defense is still sound. The defenders, although they are farther apart, have all kept their proper spacing with each other. Although they are farther apart, the time that is required for the ball to travel the extra distance will permit the defenders to cover the space between them.

In Figure 53, the defensive right halfback has taken the wrong route, causing a large gap in the secondary and we are extremely vulnerable should a pass be thrown into the area where the rubber band has broken.

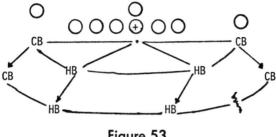

Figure 53

The 4-Spoke Alignment

Figure 54 illustrates the depth and width of the secondary defenders in the 4-spoke defensive alignment when the ball is in the middle of the field between the hash marks. The defensive corner man will line up about four yards wide and about two and one-half yards deep. They key or read the offensive halfback closest to them, and the nearest end. The reaction of the corner man will be determined by his keys (offensive end and near halfback). He will "read" the following situations:

1. If the end blocks in and the backs come toward the corner man, he should come up and contain the play quickly.
2. If the end comes out and does not block and the backs start toward the corner man, he should turn to his outside, sprint back eight yards and get set to cover his short one-quarter area.
3. If the end comes out and does not block and the back starts away from the defensive corner man, he should sprint back and get in a position to cover the deep one-third zone.

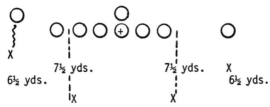

Figure 54

Cloud Coverage

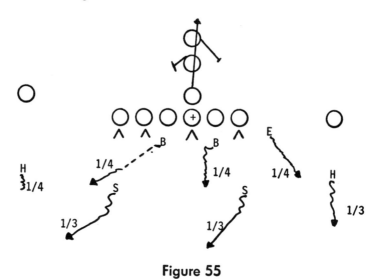

Figure 55

Defensive Left Corner—On snap of the ball, he will key for a run or pass. When he sees a pass develop, he will get ready to hit the wing as he comes down field and play the short one-quarter area. He does not want to get too deep, about 10 yards, because he must be able to come up and play the screen. If no one is in his short area, he can drift to about 12-13 yards deep.

Defensive Left Safety—After reading for his run key and recognizing a pass, he must go fast to get in the middle of his deep one-third area. He cannot assume the corner will hit the wing, so he must take off to go deep as quickly as the wing does. Once he gets to his area, he will watch the quarterback and "feel" the receiver. He cannot break on anticipation but must wait until the ball is in the air before he goes. His responsibility is deep outside one-third.

Defensive Right Safety—After taking his proper keys and recognizing a pass, he must start immediately to the deep middle one-third of the field. He will now become the safety and even if his responsibility is the middle one-third, we expect him to go from sideline to sideline.

Defensive Right Corner—After reading his keys and recognizing a pass, he will drop back to his inside and try to stay in a backpedal to cover his deep one-third. He will have short help from the weak-side end and inside linebacker, but he cannot break too fast on a sideline route because of the sideline and go. His primary responsibility is deep one-third, but he plays the wide receiver as close to man to man as he can.

Defensive Left Linebacker—When he recognizes a pass, he will sprint to his outside and back at about a 45 degree angle. When he gets to the spot where the tight end lined up, he will go back to a depth of about 12 yards. He will watch the quarterback and break off his intentions. He has a short one-quarter area responsibility and must cover the ground between the strong cornerback and the weak-side linebacker.

Defensive Right Linebacker—After keying for his run responsibility, he takes a step to his inside and then gets about 12-15 yards depth. He will be in the area where the tight end will sometimes be. He will be in an area to help out if the wide receiver breaks inside and runs a deep in route. His responsibility is the short one-quarter.

Defensive Right End—When there is no tight end to his side and the pass is a drop-back pass, his responsibility becomes the short outside one-quarter. He is working for an area about 10 yards deep and he will break off the intentions of the quarterback. He does not want to get too deep because he must come up and help on the screen pass.

Sky Coverage

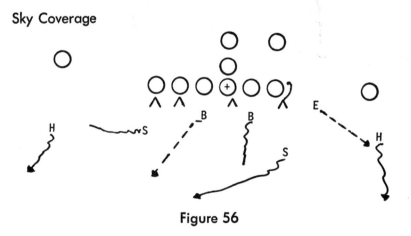

Figure 56

The only difference in the sky coverage and the cloud coverage is that the strong-side cornerback and the strong-side safety will change responsibilities. If a run occurs, the safety will be the contain man instead of the cornerback.

Pass Responsibilities for Sky Coverage

Left Cornerback—Deep one-third.
Left Safety—Short one-quarter area.
Right Safety—Zone middle one-third.
Right Cornerback—Deep outside one-third.
Left Linebacker—Short one-quarter zone.
Right Linebacker—Short one-quarter zone.
Right End—Short outside one-quarter area.

Revolve Weak

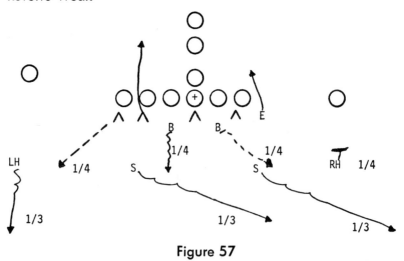

Figure 57

When we predetermine, we want to revolve to the weak side and eliminate the wide receiver to the weak side. We call this a revolve weak. This says that on a backup pass or a pass of any kind, this is what we will do.

Right Halfback—His responsibility is the short one-quarter area. He will try to knock the split receiver off of his route and at the same time, be responsible for the short outside one-quarter.
Right Safety—His responsibility is the deep outside one-third. He cannot assume the cornerback will slow the wide receiver down much, so he must take off in a hurry. After he gets in the middle of his area, he can get into a backpedal. He will not break for the ball until after it is in the air.

Left Safety—The left safety's pass responsibility is the deep middle one-third. He becomes the free safety or the "center-fielder."

Left Cornerback—His pass responsibility becomes the deep one-third to his side of the field. He thinks man-to-man as much as he can without getting beat on a corner route. He cannot expect too much help from the left end but will get some. The main thought is he knows that he does have some middle one-third help.

Left End—Regardless of who is playing this position, he must be able to play some pass defense. His particular technique on this coverage is the outside short area. He cannot spend too much time jamming the tight end because if he is to the wide side of the field, he has a long way to go. He will be a little slower setting up than the other linebackers.

Left Linebacker—After playing his run keys, he must come back to his outside and as he is trying to get 12-14 yards deep, he must be conscious of the tight end who can work into his area. He is still breaking off the quarterback's intentions, but he cannot over-play too wide.

Right Linebacker—His responsibility is the short one-quarter area, but this area will change a little because of the hashmarks. His rule of thumb is 12-14 yards deep behind where he lined up. He does not want to work too wide toward the split end.

Thunder Coverage

If we want to change up our coverage on the strong side, we call it Sky, as illustrated in Figure 56. If we want to change up our coverage on the weak side, we call it Thunder, as illustrated in Figure 58. This says we will ask the weak safety and weak-side cornerback to change assignments, and everyone else will play the same thing as revolve weak.

Pass responsibilities for thunder coverage are:

Left Halfback—Technique deep outside one-third.
Left Safety—Technique deep middle one-third.
Right Safety—Technique short outside one-quarter.
Right Halfback—Technique deep outside one-third.
Left End—Technique outside one-quarter.
Left Linebacker—Technique short one-quarter.
Right Linebacker—Technique short one-quarter.

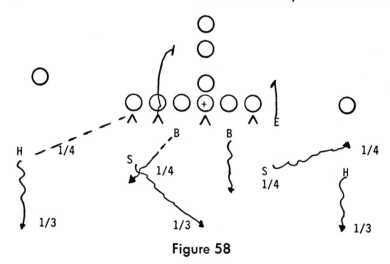

Figure 58

Man-to-Man Free Safety

At times, we want to play a man-to-man coverage and have a free safety so we just call man. This tells us we will cover our people as close as possible but we still have a free safety (this gives us a little feeling of security). Quite often, the quarterbacks are taught how to defeat zone coverages, so we always go into a game with the capability of playing man-to-man. (See Figure 59.)

Pass Responsibilities for Man-to-Man Free Safety

Strong Halfback—Pass technique, man-to-man wing.
Strong Safety—Pass technique, man-to-man X.
Weak Safety—Zone middle.

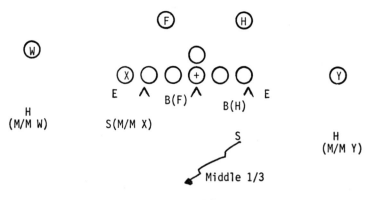

Figure 59

Weak Halfback—Man-to-man Y.
Left Linebacker—Man-to-man fullback.
Right Linebacker—Man-to-man halfback.

Double Wide Receiver

There are times when we want to double a wide receiver and still play man-to-man with the other defenders. The disadvantage of this is that we are playing a man coverage and we do not have a blitz called or a free safety, but the advantage is that we can eliminate their wide receiver when he is to the weak side.

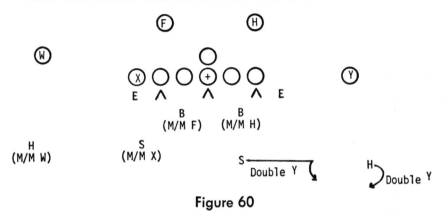

Figure 60

Pass Responsibilities for Double Y

Strong Halfback—Pass technique is man-to-man inside on wing. C.P.—No post help.
Strong Safety—Pass technique is man-to-man X.
Weak Safety—Pass technique is double Y with weak halfback.
Weak Halfback—Pass technique is to double Y with weak safety.
Left Linebacker—Pass technique is man-to-man fullback.
Right Linebacker—Pass technique is man-to-man halfback.

Blitz

There are times when we want to put pressure on the quarterback by blitzing one or more people and when we do, the pass coverage is man-to-man and no help anywhere. This is illustrated in Figure 61. We do not do this often because there is always the chance of getting hurt by the big play. We will use this only occa-

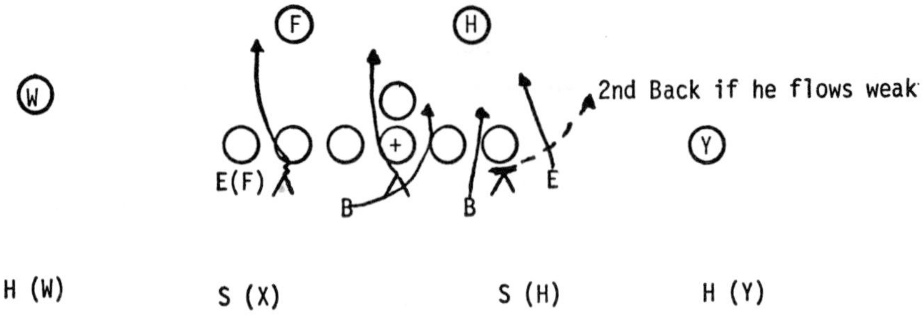

Ⓕ Ⓗ

Ⓦ 2nd Back if he flows weak

E(F) Ⓨ

B   B   E

H (W)   S (X)   S (H)   H (Y)

Figure 61

sionally, but when we blitz, we go to trap the quarterback. The responsibilities and techniques are simple, but we cannot let the quarterback have much time because the secondary people are really under pressure.

Pass Responsibilities for Blitz

> *Strong Halfback*—Man-to-man W inside.
> *Strong Safety*—Man-to-man X inside.
> *Weak Safety*—Man-to-man halfback inside.
> *Weak Halfback*—Man-to-man Y inside.
> *Strong-side End*—Man-to-man fullback.
> *Weak Tackle*—Second back, if he flows weak.

Change-up

A possible blitz change-up is to blitz the strong-side end inside the tackle, as illustrated in Figure 62. When we do this, we ask the strong-side linebacker to cover the fullback man-to-man.

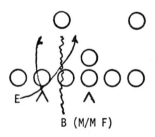

B (M/M F)

Figure 62

5 Short, 2 Deep Zone

We will play the 5 short, 2 deep two different ways as illustrated in Figures 63, 64, and 65. It depends on what the opponent is trying to do. The 4 deep people play the same on both of them. The change occurs depending upon which end rushes and when the end drops off. There will also be a change in direction the linebackers drop.

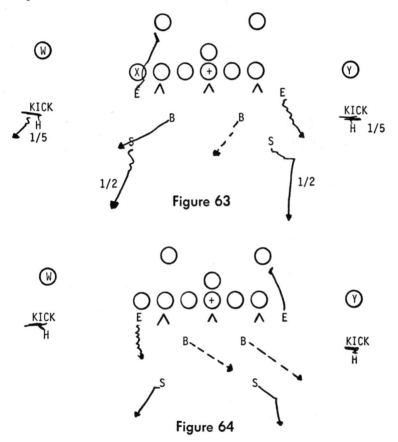

Figure 63

Figure 64

Pass Responsibilities for 5 Short 2 Deep Zone

Cornerbacks—Pass technique is to kick the receiver and play short one-fifth.

Safeties—Pass technique is one-half of the field. They must get depth and width fast.

Linebackers and Defensive Ends—Regardless of which direction they are dropping, the technique calls for a short one-fifth.

The weakness of this coverage is a tight end fast down the middle and the wide receivers on a fade route about 23 yards deep. It is a "must" to get a good kick on the outside receivers.

5 Short, 2 Deep Man

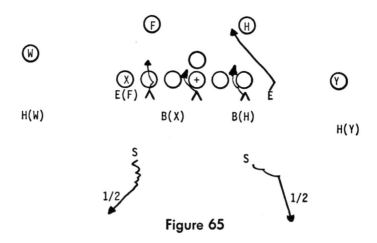

Figure 65

Pass Responsibilities for 5 Short, 2 Deep Man

Strong Halfback—Pass technique is man-to-man wing inside.
Strong Safety—Pass technique is ½ field.
Weak Safety—Pass technique is ½ field.
Weak Halfback—Pass technique is man-to-man Y inside.
Strong Linebacker—Pass technique is man-to-man X.
Strong End—Pass technique is man-to-man fullback.
Weak Linebacker—Pass technique is man-to-man halfback.

The weakness of this coverage is the possibility of some type of quarterback draw.

CONCLUSION

We have tried to show the 5-spoke, 3 deep concept, the 4-spoke and revolve concept, some man-to-man coverages, blitz and also some 5 short, 2 deep with a man underneath and zone underneath. Regardless of what kind of pass defense you play, there is one thing that is important and that is for your secondary people to perfect several techniques; then you can play a maximum of coverages with a minimum of communication. Be good in this area, work it every day and remember that confidence is important, and confidence comes from doing something right over and over.

CHAPTER 6

Our Kicking Game
Techniques

THE OVERALL KICKING GAME IS PROBABLY THE MOST IMPORTANT PHASE of football. In considering the work to be done on the practice field, I probably place more emphasis upon the kicking game than any other coach. I feel I cannot have a sound football team unless we have an extremely sound kicking game. You will win or lose with the kicking game.

THE PUNTING GAME

I am certain our players are "sold" on the kicking game, and take pride in it. If a player takes pride in something, he will do it well. Incidentally, we work on our kicking game every Tuesday during the regular season. Previously, we waited until Thursday to work on our kicking game, but we found our players were tired the day of the football game, probably as a result of so much running on Thursday. We use the kicking together with our kick-return game in our pre-season practice as a conditioner. We feel we can get sufficient running from our kicking game to get our players in good physical condition. At the same time we are developing this important phase of the game.

The Punter

Instead of merely talking to our players about their individual kicking game assignments, we go on the field and rehearse everything over and over again. This is also true of any unusual situation that might confront the punter at various times during the game. We also time our punters. I believe, however, it is possible to over-coach the kickers, and this is not desirable. I know from past experience. When we tried too thoroughly to coach our kickers, we found we were probably doing more harm than good. At least, we were not getting the desired results in comparison to the amount of time we were devoting to their instruction. As an illustration, I had Bob Gain at Kentucky, an All-American tackle, who as a freshman was a terrific kick-off man. By taking only three steps, he could boot the ball out of the end zone when he kicked off. Unfortunately, we over-coached him and by the time he was a senior he would run 10 yards on his approach, and could only kick the ball 35 yards on the kick-off.

Another illustration relates to Clayton Webb, a very fine punter whom I had at the University of Kentucky. As a freshman, he could "hang" the ball in the air for a relatively long period of time when he punted. Yet during his senior year I felt we had coached him down to a 29.4-yard average on his punts. Consequently, we now do very little coaching of the kickers.

We like to have our punters use the step-and-a-half method, taking the first (half) step with the kicking foot, then a full step with the nonkicking foot. We ask our punters to hold the ball 18 inches in front of the hip over their kicking foot. We watch our kickers closely, time them, and try not to over-coach them if they are kicking well in practice. However, we do have a meeting with our kickers to review every situation that might confront them in a game. We want our punters to know what to do under such conditions, always taking into consideration the tactical situation. Merely talking about these problems is not sufficient training for the punters. They must be placed in various confronting situations and must have the opportunity to react to them on the practice field if they are to perform with proficiency in a game. An example will illustrate my point.

One of my former assistants at the University of Kentucky played under an extremely intelligent football coach, a Phi Beta Kappa honors graduate. The coach had gone over many situations on the blackboard, but had never taken time to actually rehearse them under game-like conditions. This was a typical situation: Assuming that a team had the lead in the game, and on third down, the team was forced to kick from behind its own goal line, if the punter received a poor snap from his center and was unable to kick, he should pick up the football and either run with it or throw an incomplete forward pass. The team was playing Michigan State, and leading 7-6 in the fourth quarter. The team was backed up to its own 2-yard line. The punter said, as he lined up to punt, that he knew exactly what to do if he received a bad pass from his center. The pass was poor, the punter picked up the ball and threw it up into the stands. Unfortunately, the play was not an incomplete forward pass, but was ruled a safety as the ball went out of the end zone behind the goal line, and Michigan State won, 8-7. I am not criticizing the punter or his coach as both are extremely capable men, but merely citing what can occur if a kicker is merely told what to do but is not given actual experience under game-like conditions practicing it.

Our procedure is to put the ball on our 2-yard line, inform our kicker of what could occur, then give him the "works." We load up and rush hard, give him a bad pass, etc., and our punter must react properly to the situation, always being aware of the tactical situation.

Since I have been coaching, one of the few punts we have had blocked was at Texas A&M when we were playing Rice Institute. The situation was as follows: third down, senior punter, poor pass from center. Instead of attempting to run with the ball, since we still had fourth down in which to kick, my punter tried to kick. The result was a blocked punt. In fairness to the player, I must assume the responsibility for the blocked punt. We had not done a good job of coaching the punter since he did not react to the situation properly. Nevertheless, the mistake was costly.

The Center

The most important person in our kicking game is our center. We believe that if he can snap the ball back to our punter at a distance of 13 yards with a perfect pass in six-tenths of a second, we won't get our kicks blocked. I believe about 98 percent of all blocked kicks have resulted from imperfect passes from the center to the kicker. Incidentally, as a coaching point, if the center makes a poor pass, your kicker should inform him of this.

In timing the center's pass, we have had very few centers who could snap the ball in less than six-tenths of a second. I recall, however, there was a center at the University of Georgia who could get the ball back to the kicker in four-tenths of a second. This is the exception, however, rather than the rule.

We time our centers in their work every day. As a point of interest, the coaches are not with the centers when we are timing them. We put a defensive man over our centers as we want our centers to pass the ball and then block a man, rather than keep their heads down, watching the ball going back to the punter.

Timing the Punter

We want our punters to get the ball away within one and three-tenths seconds from the time the ball hits their hands on the pass from center, until their foot makes contact with the ball. Gene Henderson, one of my kickers at Texas A&M, could get the ball away in one second. Babe Parelli at Kentucky could also get the ball away in a second when punting. Here once again these are more exceptions and not the rule.

I stated previously we wanted our kickers to use the step-and-one-half method of punting. We are not too concerned if he doesn't follow this method, providing he kicks well. Nor are we too concerned about his method of holding and dropping the ball and other individual techniques, providing he kicks well and gets the ball away in one and three-tenths seconds or less. If our kicker is a 3-step kicker, who kicks well and can get the ball off in the prescribed time limit, we merely move him back an extra yard. Frankly, we don't believe we'll ever get a kick blocked if the center gets the ball back in six-tenths of a second or less, and the kicker's time does not exceed one and three-tenths seconds (total time of one and nine-tenths seconds), providing the defensive men are bumped and not permitted to have a straight run directly at the kicker.

When talking about the punting game, one must realize the importance of the length of time the ball is in the air over the field of play. We want our kicker to be able to kick the ball so that it will remain up in the air and over the playing field for a period of four seconds or more. Consequently, a kick of four seconds' duration in flight will be about a 40-yard punt. We are not interested in an 80-yard punt, as we cannot adequately cover such a long kick. The following example will illustrate my point.

I had a player at one time who could literally kick the football a country mile. Yet his kicking was very erratic. I recall he kicked the football 78 yards out-of-bounds in a game against Tennessee, and later in the fourth quarter he kicked the ball 80 yards over the end zone line. In another football game, he kicked the ball 70 yards, out-kicking his coverage, and the opposition returned it for the game-winning touchdown against us. My point is that he was too good a kicker for us. The average net gain is the most important thing in punting, not the total distance the punter kicks the ball. A punt 40 yards from the line of scrimmage with no return is a 40-yard kick. A 60-yard punt returned 50 yards is a net punt of 10 yards. We are interested only in the net gain of the play.

If the kicked ball can remain in the air for four seconds and if it takes one and nine-tenths seconds to get the punt away, there is a total period of time of five and nine-tenths seconds expended. If our linemen block for one second on the line before releasing to cover the punt, they will have approximately four and nine-tenths seconds to cover the ball. A fast lineman can get downfield a good distance in four and nine-tenths seconds, though I don't know of anyone who can cover 60 or 70 yards in this period of time. As you can see, this sort of thing allows a team time to get the ball, set up a wall, get a couple of key blocks and run one back for a long gain or a touchdown merely because the punter has out-kicked his coverage. Therefore, we are not interested in how far the punter kicks the ball, but we are vitally interested in how far the opposition returns our punts. I shall discuss this particular phase of the kicking game in greater detail shortly.

Practicing the Punting Game

During the regular scheduled practices, we work on our defensive kick-game game at least one period two days a week, and sometimes three days a week. These periods never have a time limit, and they are our last drill. Our reasoning is two-fold. First, the players are tired and in order to get proper execution and coverage, we insist they give that "little extra," which I feel is so important in order to build a winner. Second, the men know there is no time limit and we are going to work on this phase of our football program until we do it to my satisfaction. Therefore, they strive extra hard to get perfect execution and coverage so we can end practice. We feel if the players can learn to execute the kicking game perfectly while they are tired, they will do it perfectly during the actual game.

Spread Punt Line Splits

The main advantage of using spread punt formation is that the defensive team has a difficult time holding up your coverage. A team can cover its punt much wider. If a team can spread its men across the field as they are covering a kick, it is very hard for the receiving team to return the ball for a sizable gain.

The splits in our offensive line are determined largely by the size of the men. We want our guards to be split about one and one-half yards from the center. These splits also will be determined by the physical size of our backfield men whom we place in the gaps to each side of the center, two yards deep. If the back is a small man, then the guard will cut down his split to approximately one yard. Conversely, if the back is a large person, the guard can widen his split to approximately one and one-half yards. Our tackles will split from their guards one and one-half to two yards. Each tackle must be able to block the second man outside of his guard. Our ends can split out as far as they wish, providing they can block back all the way to the tackle if a situation arises warranting it. The ends usually split out about two yards, as illustrated in Figure 66.

Our up-backs line up in the seams between the guard and center, about two yards deep, as was explained previously. The personal protector will line up five yards deep, and will be on the right side for a right-footed kicker, and on the left for a left-footed kicker. His depth will be 13 yards. The type of spread punt we employ is illustrated in Figure 66.

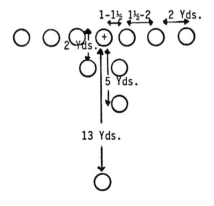

Figure 66

Spread Punt Blocking Rules

We do not believe a defensive lineman will ever get a straight run at the spot where the kicker's foot meets the football if our players occupy their proper positions, unless the defensive man comes from the outside of our protection. For this reason, we feel it is not necessary for our players to block for more than a second before going down under the punt. Our players are instructed to count, "One thousand and three," then release downfield covering the kick.

The rules which our players use in protecting our punter apply to the blocking of any man who is within one yard of the line of scrimmage. We do not feel an opposing player can block a kick if he is more than one yard off the line of scrimmage, even though we do not block him. Our spread punt blocking rules are as follows:

Center—The center should make a perfect pass to the kicker, snap up his head quickly, and cover the kick immediately. We do not ask him to block anyone.

Guards—Our guards will block the first man to their outside, and they must keep the inside foot stationary. If a guard steps laterally with his inside foot as he blocks, he will leave a hole through which a defensive man can sprint and block the kick. After he has blocked the first man to his outside for a period of one second, which I explained above, he covers the kick downfield.

Tackles—If there are two men lined up between the tackle and his adjacent guard, he will block to his inside. If there aren't two men between his position and his adjacent guard, he will block the first man to his outside. After he has blocked for one second, he will cover the kick.

Ends—Each end will block the first man to his outside, unless there are two defensive men between him and his adjacent tackle. If there are two men between his guard and tackle, he will block the first man to his inside.

Up-Backs—The up-backs block anyone coming over their territory between the guard and center. If no one comes through their territory, they delay slightly and cover the kick.

Personal Protector—He looks up and down the line for the most dangerous man to the kicker, and then blocks him as he rushes.

These spread punt blocking rules apply to any defense and provide the most protection at the spot where the ball will be kicked. The basic principle for the linemen in carrying out their assignments is never to move the inside foot. If the lineman makes contact with the defensive man and throws him off-balance, then he can cover the kick immediately. The up-backs take a good stance with a wide base and uncoil at anyone coming through the inside gaps. The personal protector can use any type of block he wishes, but we prefer the butt block or the cross-body block when protecting the kicker.

Spread Punt Coverage

We want the first man down under the punt to go aggressively at the safety man's chest, really "unloading" on him if possible. He may leave his feet in order to accomplish his objective. For illustrative purposes (Figure 67), let's assume that our center is the first man down under the punt. We want him to try to beat the football down the field, and tackle the safety man high when he touches it, or force the safety man to fair-catch the football. We want our guards to go down and assume positions indicated in Figure 67. Our left end and right tackle will go down and set up five yards outside of the safety man, and five yards away from him. We set our right end out about 10 yards, and he is our "sprinter." His assignment is to sprint straight for the safety man, and force the safety to fumble the ball, if possible. His line of direction has a second purpose, too. Since he is in an excellent position to catch the football should the punter fake the punt and pass, the defense must adjust to him and cannot merely permit him to run a diagonal course downfield every time we have a punting situation. If the defense continuously ignores him and doesn't adjust to him when he covers punts, sooner or later we are going to hit him with the pass for a sizable gain.

It is not possible for a coach to get the type of coverage on kicks, as illustrated in Figure 67, unless he stresses the fact to his players that it is extremely important for them to spread out in order to maintain proper positions in "spreading the net" for the receiver. They must sprint at top speed in covering kicks. We do not want our left end and right tackle to make any tackles in our punt coverage, as they merely turn the runner into the other men. We want our six men to go down and get set in a football position three yards from the football and then guard the safety man. In assuming a good football position, we mean a position in which the player's eyes are on the safety man, his tail is down, back straight, and his feet apart. If we have six men down on the safety man, guarding him, he will have no place to run. We want to drive the safety man back and forth, searching for a place to turn upfield, and then we'll move in on him. We refer to this as our One-Six Formation. We want our up-backs to go downfield and take the positions of linebackers behind our six-man coverage, as illustrated in Figure 67. They must be in a position to defend against the return up the middle. We want our personal protector and punter to take halfback positions to the outside behind the one-six-two coverage formation (Figure 67).

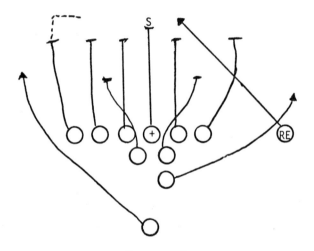

Figure 67

We spend a great deal of time giving our players practice in executing their assignments on blocking and covering from spread punt formation. I can assure you that merely talking about their assignments and responsibilities will not obtain the desired results. I think we do a good job of covering punts simply because we work on this important phase of the kicking game so much.

As I mentioned previously, we do our kicking work last, not setting a definite time limit on it. When our players are covering punts, we blow a whistle and everyone stops. We want to find the players in their proper positions when covering the kick. If they are not covering to our satisfaction, we merely do it over and over again until we get the type of coverage we want. The players actually put the pressure on each other to get perfect coverage, consequently we generally spend about 10 minutes instead of 20 minutes covering punts.

OUR TIGHT PUNT FORMATION

The only time we kick from a tight punt formation is when we are backed up inside our own 3-yard line and it is impossible for us to kick from a spread formation since our kicker cannot get the sufficient depth of 13 yards which we think is necessary. Therefore, we always tell our quarterback we should never kick the ball from behind our own 3-yard line. His objective is to get us out to at least the 3-yard line so we can employ spread punt. Assuming we can't get out to the 3-yard line, then we will have to use tight punt formation. When we are definitely going to kick the ball out-of-bounds as we do on occasion, we kick from tight formation.

Because I feel we cannot cover the kick very well from tight punt formation, the quarterback will always designate in the huddle the direction the punter is going to kick the ball—"Punt from tight punt; kick to our right." This tells our linemen in which direction they should sprint after they have blocked their men. It also affects the blocking assignments of our ends. Figure 68 illustrates our tight punt formation and coverage on a kick to our right. Our blocking rules are as follows:

Interior Linemen—Our interior linemen will line up in a tight formation with very little splits. They all have one blocking rule— inside gap N/T over, which means they will block a man if he is in their inside gap; if there is no one playing that position, they will block the man playing over them. They must all block for one and one-half counts, when using the tight punt, then release and cover the kick quickly.

Ends—The ends will be split out about two yards, and they have definite assignments. If the quarterback indicates in the huddle the kick will be to the right, then the right end does not have a blocking assignment but he must cover the kick immediately. He must get good width and make certain the ball carrier does not get

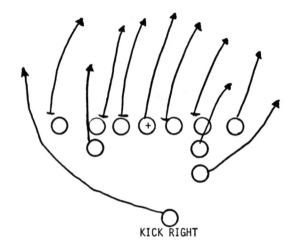

KICK RIGHT

Figure 68

outside of him. The end playing the position on the opposite side will block the defensive end. If the kick is to the left side, the ends merely exchange assignments.

Up-Backs—They will line up about two yards deep and in positions behind their respective offensive tackles. Their assignment is to keep their inside feet in place and block the first man who shows outside of our offensive tackle. They must make the defensive men come to them. They are going to protect their areas.

Personal Protector—He lines up about one and one-half yards behind the right up-back, and his assignment is to block the second man outside of our offensive tackle or the first man outside of our up-back. When he makes contact with the defensive man, he forces him to his outside. He, too, must keep his inside foot in place. If we are going to kick the ball to our left after the ball has been snapped, he will cross over and block the first man who shows outside of our left up-back. He covers wide to the side he blocks on.

Kicker—The kicker is back nine yards, and after he kicks, he immediately covers to the side opposite where he kicked the ball.

The tight punt coverage is practically the same as we use on our spread punt, but the linemen are so close together it is difficult for them to cover wide. Our center cannot leave quite as quickly as on spread punt and we hold our blocks a little longer. Otherwise, everything is the same on the two punt formations.

OUR QUICK KICK FORMATION

The quick kick is a tremendous offensive weapon which we now employ less frequently than we did when our players played both ways. We think the quick kick has helped us win a few football games in the past, and I suspect it will continue to aid us in the future if we execute it properly. Consequently we will continue to spend time practicing and coaching the quick kick. A team that quick kicks frequently makes its short passing game more effective as its opponents must play their safety man deeper than usual.

We try not to tip off when we intend to quick kick. We try to make the formation look exactly like our regular running formation. One slight difference is that we line up our backs slightly deeper than usual and slightly to their right, as illustrated in Figure 69, if the left halfback is quick kicking.

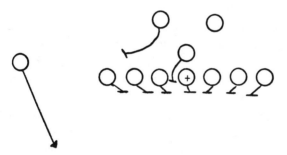

Figure 69

Quick Kick Rules and Coverage

Our quick kick rules and coverage are very simple, and are as follows:

Ends, Guards, and Tackles—They block the man on their inside gap, and if no man is there, they block the man over them. They are trying to form a completely new line of scrimmage on their first charge about one yard straight ahead. It is very important these six men penetrate the defense on their initial charge, in order to give the kicker adequate room to kick the football.

Center—The center's first responsibility is to make a good snap to the person who is going to kick the football. Then he blocks the man in the off-gap—no one there, he blocks the man over him. As an example, if we have a right-footed kicker, the center will block to his left, as illustrated in Figure 69. If the kicker is left-footed, the center would block to his right.

Quarterback—The quarterback acts as if he is going to receive a hand-back pass from his center. However, he takes a wider leg spread than usual in order to permit the center to pass the ball directly through the quarterback's legs to his left halfback (Figure 69). His blocking rule is to block the on-gap, i.e., the right gap for a right-footed kicker, as illustrated in Figure 69, and the left gap for a left-footed kicker.

Wing—He has no blocking assignment as he covers the quick kick immediately.

Fullback—He will move over to his right slightly, and his assignment is to block the first man who shows outside of our offensive right end. He will step up to meet him, giving the kicker adequate room to kick the ball.

Left Halfback or Kicker—He lines up a little deeper than usual and moves over about a foot to his right. When the kicker catches the football, he will rock his weight back to his right foot, leaving his left foot in place, and pivoting his body to the right. He then takes a step with his left foot in about a 45 degree angle to the sideline, and at the same time he will drop the ball (pointing straight down the field) and kick the ball trying to make contact with it over the arch of his right foot. After he hits the football, he leg-swings toward the goal line. This action will make the ball go end-over-end and cause it to continue rolling toward the goal line upon hitting the ground.

The quick kick must come as a complete surprise to the defense or it will not be effective. If the defense knows you are going to quick kick, it will be more effective to employ spread punt and kick the football. You will get better protection and coverage from spread formation, though the element of surprise is not present.

OUR PUNT RETURN

We have never done what I would consider an outstanding job of returning our opposition's punts. One reason for this is that it is awfully easy to overlook this particular phase of the kicking game.

We feel about punt returns about the same as we do pass defense—you must either rush or return, and it is difficult to accomplish both at the same time. Therefore, we try to do one or the other, depending upon the game situation.

We use a punt return to our left and one to our right, and a return up the middle to keep the kicking team honest. All of these returns have proven satisfactory from time to time.

Punt Return Left

When we are going to return the punt left or right, we line up in a strong side defense. Consequently, there is no indication of whether we are returning the punt right or left, or rushing the punter trying to block the punt.

Figure 70 illustrates our punt return left. Our return rules are as follows:

Left End—He comes across the line of scrimmage about five yards deep into the offensive backfield, and makes certain the kicker does not get outside of him in the event the latter tries to run with the ball. After he sees the kicker punt the football, he turns and swings in behind his right guard in forming the wall. He will be the fourth man in line and he must keep his proper distance from his guard. The length of the kick will determine how far downfield he will go before he sets up. He blocks anyone who is in his area trying to break through the wall.

We have an imaginary post three yards outside of our defensive left end, and we want all of our players to swing wide and go around this spot before going back downfield. If all of the players do this, our entire line will be running in approximately the same path and our wall will be set up correctly.

Left Tackle—As soon as he crosses the line of scrimmage, he will turn to his left, go around the imaginary post, and head quickly downfield becoming the first man in the wall. His block will be a key one, springing loose the safety man. His depth depends on the distance the punter kicks the ball.

Middle Guard—He follows the same course as the left tackle. He will be the second man in the wall, and he must maintain the proper distance between the first man and himself. When he gets into position, he will block anyone who is in his area trying to break through the wall.

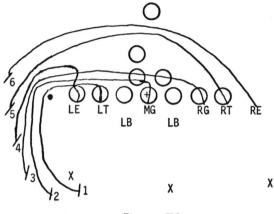

Figure 70

Right Guard—Same course as the left tackle, only he follows the middle guard around the imaginary post and back downfield becoming the third man in the wall. He should keep his proper distance from our middle guard.

Right Tackle—He will rush the punter from the outside, making certain the punter actually kicks the ball. Then turning to his left, he will swing wide, as illustrated in Figure 70, becoming the fifth man in the wall. He must keep his proper distance from our defensive left end who will be the fourth man, as I explained previously.

Right End—He will rush the kicker from the outside making certain he actually kicks the ball. He will then turn to his left, and start around the imaginary post. He will be the sixth man in the wall, and he should maintain a proper distance between his right tackle and himself.

Right Linebacker—The right linebacker will come back to his outside and block the most dangerous pursuer threatening the safety man. He usually blocks the offensive left end as he covers the punt downfield.

Left Linebacker—He will come back fast to his outside, and his responsibility is to block out the offensive right end. The others are blocking toward the wide side of the field. He is the only man blocking toward the sideline.

Halfbacks—They will handle the short kick to their side of the field. Otherwise they are personal protectors for the safety man if he fields the kick. They block the most dangerous pursuer who is in a position to tackle our receiver.

Safety—It is very important that the ball is handled in the air and not permitted to strike the ground and bounce around. Assuming the safety man catches the football, he should start straight up the field in order to give his wall time to form and to draw the pursuers into the middle toward him. Then he swings in behind his wall on the sideline.

Our Middle Punt Return

Our return up the middle is very similar to our man-to-man kickoff return (Figure 74), in that we assign one man to block one man at the line of scrimmage. Each defensive man is supposed to stay with his offensive man, as illustrated in Figure 71. We use the same defensive alignment as when we are going to return the ball to our right or left (Figure 71).

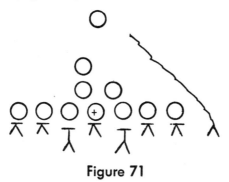

Figure 71

If we want to be in a balanced defensive alignment, and we know they have a slow offensive lineman, we will line up in a straight 6-2 defense. Figure 72 illustrates our alignment and hold-up return if we know the offensive center is slow. We merely let him go, and our interior linemen and linebackers hold up the offensive ends, tackles, and guards. Our ends rush the kicker from the outside, making certain he kicks the football. The interior linemen and linebackers use the same techniques our offensive backs use when they are protecting the passer. When they feel they are losing their men, they will go into a cross-body block. Our halfback will field the ball in the air and start upfield. If he sees a hole, he will break for it on our middle return.

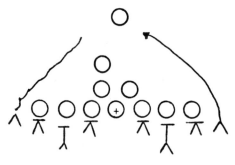

Figure 72

OUR KICK-OFF AND ITS COVERAGE

The kick-off is a very important phase of the defensive kicking game because of the number of times it is used in a game. As you know, the kick-off comes at the start of the game, at the beginning of the second half, and after a team has scored. It is a terrific advantage to get a deep kick-off with good coverage, and tackle the ball carrier inside his 20-yard line. It is important to eliminate the long run on the kick-off return for several reasons. First, a long run has a demoralizing effect on the kicking team, and gives the receiving team both a psychological and a strategical advantage. With respect to the latter point, if the receiving team gets beyond its 30-yard line, it can open up with its entire offensive attack immediately. Conversely, if the kicking team keeps the receiving team deep in its own territory, the receiving team is forced to run a limited offense, punt the ball or gamble in order to get out of its own territory.

Two Types of Kick-Offs

We employ two different kinds of kick-offs, depending upon the particular opponent we are playing. As an illustration, if we know the opposition has two dangerous runners playing deep, we will kick the ball in such a manner that it strikes the ground and bounces around making it difficult for either man to control. This tactic also gives us time to cover the kick properly. On the other hand, if our scouting report reveals the safeties are only fair runners, then we will kick the ball high in the air and end-over-end. Of course, if we had a place kicker who could boot the ball out of the end zone every time, our kick-off strategy would be simple and our problem would be solved. Kickers with such ability are difficult to locate.

I suppose our coverage on the kick-off is like that of most other football teams. We want our men back five yards from the ball in a 3-point stance, all facing toward the football. Our quarterback stands one yard to the side of the ball and a yard off the ball on the 39-yard line with his arms raised ready to give the starting signal to the men watching him. When the kicker approaching the football gets to a point where the men covering the kick-off cannot get offside, the quarterback will drop his arms as a signal for the men to start forward together. We want everyone but the safeties to cover the kick quickly. Each man is to protect his own area, and then go to the cut-off point. We instruct our ends to be certain no one gets outside of them.

We have two safeties, not including the quarterback. If the ball is kicked down the middle, the quarterback is the safety. If the ball is kicked to our right, our quarterback and left halfback will be safeties. If the ball is kicked to our left, the quarterback and our right halfback will be safeties, as illustrated in Figure 73. When our safeties drop out, our other men will converge slightly to close the gaps. The safety men cover slowly, and should always be in a position to tackle the ball carrier before he can score.

Figure 73 illustrates the fullback kicking the ball. If a player other than the fullback is the kick-off man, he and the fullback merely exchange places in the lineup.

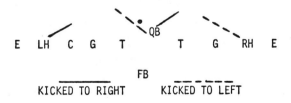

E   LH   C   G   T   QB   T   G   RH   E

FB

KICKED TO RIGHT   KICKED TO LEFT

Figure 73

It is very important that our men going down to cover the kick-off keep their proper distance from the men on each side of them. If we have two men covering the kick close together, a good block by the receiving team could eliminate both of them, and then our coverage would not be sound.

OUR KICK-OFF RETURN

I explained previously the advantages of returning the kick-off. I like to get this psychological and strategical "jump" on our opposition when we receive the kick-off; consequently, we attach much importance and significance to returning the kick-off. We work hard on our returns. We want a good return so that if we must surrender the ball by punting to the opposition, we'll give it to them back in their 3-down zone. By this I mean they must make a first down in their first three plays or they will be forced to kick the ball back to us on the fourth down. If we get a poor return and cannot move the ball and must punt it from deep in our own territory, we might give the ball to them immediately in their 4-down zone. Now we have increased their chances of scoring by 25 percent merely because we did not get a good kick-off return.

Our Kick-Off Return Right

Figure 74 illustrates our kick-off return to our right with the men on the receiving team blocking their "numbers" downfield, as indicated. Each man on the kicking team is numbered from one through seven from the outside-in, except the last four men on the opposite side of the kicking line, i.e., the men on our extreme left in Figure 74. If we know from scouting reports who the safety man will be, we do not give him a number. If we don't know who the safety man is, we instruct our players—if your man turns out to be a safety, regardless of where you line up, then you will block the first man to your inside. The deep back who does not receive the ball will head upfield and block the most dangerous man threatening the ball carrier.

Our Middle Kick-Off Return

We think our middle kick-off return is very simple and actually takes very little work to perfect it. What we are trying to accomplish is to wall off the opposition in a solid line. This gives our ball carrier time to pick up speed and we let him break where the hole opens up.

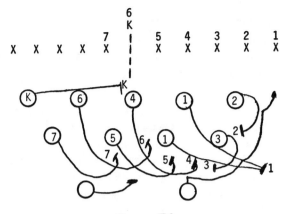

Figure 74

In our alignment, illustrated in Figure 75, our front line is about 12 yards in front of our back line. When the ball is kicked, our front line will drop back six yards and get into a good football position, keeping their eyes on the men they are going to block. When we are using this type of return, we commence counting from the outside-in on both ends of the line. The end men are not blocked because we know they are taught to stay outside. If our scouting report shows they converge and other men cover the outside, then we will change our assignments to handle the situation.

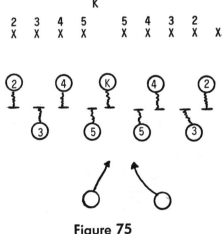

Figure 75

We want our blockers to use the same block that our backs use when protecting the passer. We want them to remain on their feet until they feel they are losing their man. Then they go into a shield block. The deep back who does not field the ball will get in front of the ball carrier and lead interference. The back who receives the kick-off will start straight up the field attempting to gain as much yardage as possible. When he sees daylight in the line in front of it, he breaks for the opening at his discretion.

If the kicking team places the football on the hashmark to kick-off and we are employing a middle return, we will count the end man closest to the football and block him, and disregard the two farthest men from the ball on the opposite end of the line.

OUR ON-SIDE (SHORT) KICK

The on-side kick, i.e., legal short kick, is one of the best weapons a team can have when you must gain possession of the ball after a touchdown. We work on the on-side kick, practicing it every week. If an on-side kick helps us to win one football game, then it is well worth all the time we have spent on it.

Previously, I mentioned our 1955 game with Rice where we were behind 12-0, with three minutes remaining to play in the game. We scored on a running play, kicked the extra point, and with the score 12-7 we still needed a touchdown to win the football game. Having rehearsed the on-side kick during the week, as we lined up for the kick-off, we knew our strategy would be a short kick. We recovered the ball successfully on the on-side kick, then scored with a long pass, and converted the point-after-touchdown, making the score 14-12. Rice attempted to get back into the game by passing as time was running out. We intercepted a pass, scored again, and won the game 20-12. You can see why we are firm believers in the on-side kick.

Figure 76 illustrates our on-side kick to the left. We line up in our regular kick-off alignment. When the kicker approaches the ball, instead of driving through with the toe of his kicking shoe, he kicks the football with his instep. He merely tries to get a piece of the ball, sort of punching it left or right so we can go down and cover it quickly. The end, tackle and center (Figure 76) do not try to recover the ball, but try to wedge in front of it and wall off the area so the men on the receiving team cannot get possession of the football. Our halfback comes down fast and his assignment is to recover the football (behind the wall). When we kick the ball to the left, as illustrated in Figure 76, the quarterback will swing in behind the halfback in the event he misses recovering the ball and the opposition is trying to advance the kick-off.

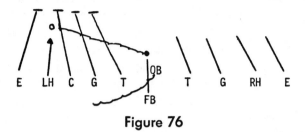

Figure 76

We also try an on-side kick down the middle with the tackles and guards (see Figure 76) forming a wall in front of the kicker, who tries to recover the football.

When we try an on-side kick to our right, the principles are the same with our end, guard and tackle forming the wall while the right halfback tries to recover the ball.

DEFENDING AGAINST AN ON-SIDE KICK

We also work on defending against the on-side (short) kick because we know the opposition will attempt to use it against us. The last year I was at Kentucky, we were playing Cincinnati and I knew they would attempt an on-side kick. I sent 11 players into the game with the sole responsibility of recovering the kick and not permitting Cincinnati to get the football. I wish I could report that we were successful, but Cincinnati recovered its on-side kick. However, our players at least knew we had worked on defending against the on-side kick and we were not surprised when the opposition used it.

When we are expecting an on-side kick, we want to get our best ball handlers up close to the restraining line so they can field the ball. Figure 77 illustrates our receiving alignment defending against the on-side kick. Our halfbacks and quarterback are at the 45-yard line, with the fullback deep and the ends in their usual alignment.

We put our five interior linemen close to the restraining line for two reasons. First, we do not want them to handle the football. Second, we want them to block or wall off for the man who is going to field the ball. Note the halfbacks are inside of the end men on the restraining line in front of them. If the ball is kicked to our left, our front men sprint quickly to a point in front of the football where they can block the men on the kicking team before they can recover the football. The halfback on the left side is instructed not to try to advance the football, but merely to fall on it and get possession of the football. The quarterback and right halfback swing in behind the left halfback in the event he mishandles the football. If the kick were to our right, the right halfback would handle the ball with the other two backs backing up the right halfback. If the ball is kicked down the middle, we want the quarterback to fall on the ball, with the two halfbacks swinging in behind him in the event he mishandles the ball. Our five front men would block in front of the ball for their quarterback.

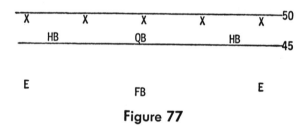

Figure 77

OUR EXTRA POINT AND FIELD GOAL PROTECTION

Our extra point and field goal protection are the same with the exception that on the latter we must cover the kick. Our point-after-touchdown and field goal attempt blocking rules are as follows:

Center—Our center's main responsibility is to make a perfect snap to the holder, and then he braces himself and holds his ground. We actually try to get our center to grab the ground with his hands so that he cannot be knocked backwards. Should the latter occur, the center would leave a hole in the line. The center must hold his ground, and he should keep both feet stationary.

Guards, Tackles, Ends—The other six linemen have exactly the same blocking rules. The guards and tackles do not take splits, so the line from tackle to tackle will be tight. The ends will split approximately six inches. None of these men can move the outside foot. It must remain stationary. They will line up looking in at the football. On the snap of the ball, the guard will step with his inside foot toward the center. He will put his head in front of the center's leg, with his neck firm against it. The guard must keep his outside leg stationary as the tackle will put his head and neck firmly against the guard's leg. The end will use the same technique putting his neck against the tackle's outside leg. We are trying to build a solid wall so the opposition cannot penetrate it and get to our kicker. We are trying to force the opponents to rush from the outside, rather than permitting them to rush inside.

Up-Backs—The up-backs line up about a yard deep and a yard inside our offensive ends. They are in a position where they can reach out and touch the tail of the end on their respective sides. The up-back's assignment is to keep his inside foot in place and force the rushers to go wide. He cannot move his inside foot, and he must not be knocked down. On a field goal attempt, he has wide responsibility to his side of the field. He will leave as soon as he hears the thud of the ball.

Holder—The holder lines up about six yards and one foot deep and his responsibility is to place the ball on the tee in a good position, permitting our kicker to get his foot into the ball.

Figure 78 illustrates our place kicking formation. The whole operation for the extra point or field goal attempt should take only one and three-tenths seconds. If it takes longer than this, it is likely the kick will be blocked.

We have our extra point and field goal kickers out 20 minutes early every day practicing their specialties. We have a set of goal posts approximately one-half as wide as the regulation width that our kickers practice kicking through.

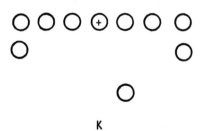

K

Figure 78

DEFENDING AGAINST A FIELD GOAL ATTEMPT

When we are trying to rush a field goal attempt, we never rush from both sides at the same time, and we always play our 3-deep pass coverage. The only exception is that our safety will line up a little deeper so he can handle the ball if the situation warrants it. We are always as conscious of the fake field goal attempt and pass as we are of the actual place kick.

We only rush from one side at a time, and it will probably be our right side if the kicker is right-footed. We overload to that side, as illustrated in Figure 79, trying to get one of our fastest ends in there to block the attempted place kick.

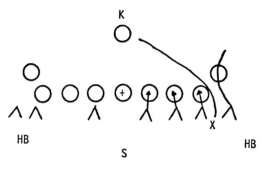

Figure 79

CONCLUSION

I think the kicking game is very important as it is tied in closely with our defensive football. You must be sound in all phases of the kicking game, as neglecting any one phase can cost you a football game. In order to have a winner, your kicking game must be sound.

CHAPTER **7**

Our Offensive
Running Game

THE MAIN OBJECTIVE OF OFFENSIVE FOOTBALL IS TO SCORE but if
for some reason we do not score, we never want to give the ball up
without a kick. In other words, in a tough game, we cannot afford to
give the ball up through a fumble or interception. We want to keep
the ball as long as possible and then punt it or kick a field goal. This
will usually force the opponent to go at least 80 yards to score and if
we play good defense, we will not lose many games.

BASIC PRINCIPLES AND REQUIREMENTS
OF OFFENSIVE FOOTBALL

Offense is based on two primary principles; running with or
passing the football. The ideal situation is to have them complement
each other. In other words, pass enough to keep the opponents off
balance and run enough to keep them off balance.

We believe here at Alabama that you must establish the running game first. We have had some outstanding passers here at
Alabama, but we always stress the importance of the running game
first.

Offense requires a lot of discipline and in order to perfect your
attack, it takes many hours of repetition. The players have assignments that must be learned, techniques that must be mastered and
everyone has to operate as a unit.

A Sound Offense

A sound offense is one in which each play is designed to gain ground and if it is executed perfectly, there is a chance for a long gainer or even a touchdown. If the offense is going to operate at maximum efficiency, the bad plays should be eliminated completely.

A sound attack will usually have the best ball carriers running behind the best blockers, but in the past few years, we have gone to the wishbone attack here at Alabama. We went to this formation for several reasons, but the main reason was that we had three good running backs and a good running quarterback, and I wanted to get them in the game at the same time. I called Darrell Royal who was coaching at the University of Texas at the time, and asked him if it would be all right if I came to Austin and spent a few days with him talking about the wishbone formation. At that time, Emory Bellard, who is presently the head coach at Mississippi State, was an assistant to Darrell and had spent quite a lot of time in developing the wishbone.

OUR OFFENSIVE TERMINOLOGY

To be sure that we are all talking the same "language" and can understand each other readily, we have adopted the following offensive terminology:

Flow—Direction in which most of the backs start.

On-Side—Lineman on side of point of attack.

Off-Side—Lineman on side away from point of attack.

Near Back—Halfback on side of flow.

Far Back—Halfback away from side of flow.

On-Back—Of the two remaining backs in the backfield, the back toward call.

Off-Back—Of the two remaining backs in the backfield, the back away from call.

Point of Attack—Spot where ball crosses the line of scrimmage.

Over—Defensive man over any part of the offensive man.

Cut Off—Shoot the head and shoulder past the defensive man, destroying his correct pursuit angle to the football.

Set—Fake pass protection block.

Slam—Entertain defensive man with shoulder and forearm.

N/T—No one there.

Position Lateral—Getting self in position to receive lateral from the man with the football.

Covered—Designates offensive man with a defensive man over him on L.O.S.

L.B.—Linebacker

M.L.B.—Middle linebacker.

L.O.S.—Line of scrimmage.

Man on L.O.S.—Defensive man down in 3- or 4-point stance on the line of scrimmage.

"6"—Right end.

"7"—Left end.

Club—A running head and shoulder block attacking the defensive man's upper extremities. This block is used in the area approaching the point of attack.

Color—First man approached with different color jersey.

Motion—Back leaving before snap of the ball.

Ice—Receiver going to outside or inside and becoming a possible receiver after making his block or when no one shows. Yell "Ice" when open.

Trail Junction Blocker—Ball carrier straddling the outside leg of junction blocker. Stay close to him.

Pursuer—Defensive man pursuing the ball carrier.

Gap—Space between two offensive men.

Flare—Call to tell a back to run a flare route.

Drive Man—Man who does the driving on a two-on-one block.

Post Man—Man who stops the progress of the defensive man on a two-on-one block.

Odd Defense—Offensive guards not covered.

Even Defense—Offensive guards covered.

Box Defense—Only two deep men in the secondary.

3-Deep Defense—Three deep men in the defensive secondary.

9-Man Front—Box defense.

8-Man Front—Three-deep defense.

Position Ball—Bring ball immediately into belly, elbows in, ball in fingers.

Drive Block—An aggressive head and shoulders block to turn opponent.

Climb Block—A running drive block.

Chop Block—Open field block on men in the secondary by throwing your body (extended) at his shoulders.

Fill—Protect the area to your inside.

Shoot Out—Springing from your original stance, hitting on your hands and feet running (used to get downfield).

Against the Grain—Direction in the secondary opposite the flow.

On Linebacker—Denotes (on-side L.B., N/T M.L.B.).

Position—Getting to a spot between the man you are to block and the ball carrier.

Eagle—Call to tackle and guard to switch assignments.

Head On—Man nose-to-nose.

Blocks and Related Calls

We ask our offensive linemen to make some calls at the line of scrimmage, so we will block each defense a little differently. What we are really doing is calling the plays in the huddle, as far as direction, flow and intent are concerned, and we let our tackles be responsible for calling the blocking scheme for the line.

Examples of these calls are:

Green—A call to tell the guard and tackle to change assignments.

Blue—A call to tell the tackle and guard to switch assignments.

Black—A call to tell the tackle and guard to block number one and number two on the weak side.

Switch—A call to tell the tackle and end to switch assignments.

Yellow—A call to tell the center to block number one technique to strong side.

Gap—A call to tell the on-guard and tackle and end to block first man to their on-side.

Over—A call to tell everyone to block down and the fullback will block number four man.

Near—A call to tell the halfback to block the first inside linebacker.

Slide—Call between the center and guard to alert for area pass protection.

Back Side—Center block away from where the play was called.

We want all of our players and coaches to understand and use our offensive terminology. One or two words either explain the descriptive action we want or identify some segment of the offense or the opposition's defense. The terms are simple, meaningful and descriptive.

OUR OFFENSIVE STANCE

The offensive stance is very important. It is difficult enough trying to attain maximum results when your players are lined up in their proper stance, but it puts them at a distinct disadvantage and handicaps them greatly if you permit them to assume a stance that is improper and incorrect. Therefore, we put first things first, and try to coach our players always to take the proper stance.

Offensive Stance for Linemen

The stance for the linemen, with the exception of the center, is basically the same, with allowances being made for various physical characteristics, which vary from individual to individual. The inside foot is forward, the feet staggered in an arch-to-toe relationship. The tackles and ends exaggerate the stagger from heel to toe since they are further removed from the center and quarterback.

The feet should not be spread wider than the individual's shoulders, with the weight of the body concentrated on the balls of the feet. The heels should be slightly in, with the cleats on the heel of the forward foot almost touching the ground. The ankles should be bent slightly. The knees should be bent slightly more than 90 degrees, and turned slightly in. The tail is even or a little higher than the shoulders, and splitting the forward and rear heels. The back is straight, shoulders square, neck relaxed, and eyes open, keeping the defensive linebacker in line of sight. The hands are placed down slightly outside of the feet, elbows relaxed, and thumbs in and slightly forward of the shoulders.

Offensive Stance for Center

The center lines up in a left-handed stance with the feet even and slightly wider than the shoulders. The weight is on the balls of the feet, heels turned slightly in, with the cleats on the heels of the shoes almost touching the ground. The knees are slightly in and bent a little more than 90 degrees. The tail is slightly higher than the shoulders and about two inches in front of the heels. The center places his left hand inside his legs down from between his eye and ear almost directly under the forehead, with the fingers spread and the thumb turned slightly in. The shoulders are square, the back is straight, the neck is relaxed, and the eyes looking upward. His right hand grasps the football like a passer. He should reach out as far as possible without changing his stance. The center is coached to place the ball on his tail as quickly as possible with a natural turn of the arm. He should drive out over the ball with his head coming up and tail down, keeping his shoulders square as he makes his hand-back to the quarterback.

Quarterback's Stance

The quarterback is coached to get into a football position with the feet slightly wider than the shoulders, weight on the balls of the feet, heels and knees turned slightly in, knees bent slightly, and a natural bend at the waist in order to be in a good position to receive the ball from the center as he snaps the ball on the hand-back. The elbows must be bent and in close to the body.

The quarterback's right hand goes up in the center's crotch. He turns it slightly to the right. At this spot, he applies pressure with the hand to his center's tail. The left hand must be in a comfortable position, making slight contact with the right hand, and it is used to trap the ball and to assist the right hand in taking the football from the center.

Halfback's Stance

The feet of the halfback should not be wider than the shoulders, and staggered in a heel-to-toe relationship with each other.

The weight should be on the balls of the feet, but will vary slightly depending upon the direction the halfback must move in carrying out his particular assignment. With the snap of the ball, he should throw himself in the direction he is going, and he should not use a crossover step.

His knees should be bent a little beyond 90 degrees, with the knees and heels turned slightly in, and the tail a little higher than the shoulders. The halfback's shoulders should be square, with his head and eyes in a position to see the defensive linebacker on the opposite side from him. The inside hand should be down, slightly forward and inside of the knee with the thumb turned a little to the inside. The body weight should be forward slightly.

Fullback's Stance

The fullback lines up with the feet even and a little wider than his shoulders. The cleats on the heels of his shoes should touch the ground. The heels and knees are turned slightly in with the weight on the balls of the feet. The head and eyes are in a relaxed position, but where they can see the second man standing outside of the offensive end. The hands are directly in front of each foot with the thumbs turned in. The shoulders are square, the back is straight, the tail is directly above the heels, with the weight slightly forward, but not to such an extent that he cannot start quickly in a lateral direction to either side.

OFFENSIVE LINE SPLITS

The use of intelligent line splits by the offensive guards, tackles and ends must be mastered in order to realize the full potential of our basic offensive attack. Without proper line splits, it is impossible for the offense to function at 100 percent efficiency. Therefore, we must present line split theory and coach our linemen so that they will have a clear understanding of why and when we want to move in, out or remain stationary. Mastering the intelligent use of line splits is one of the two most important single duties of the offensive linemen. (The other is a quick offensive charge together on the starting count.)

The Pre-Shift Position

When the linemen leave the huddle and come up to the line of scrimmage in a pre-shift position (hands on knees in a semi-upright stance), the basic split rule for the guards is to split one full man. The tackles and ends will split slightly more than one full man. As the linemen go down into their offensive stance, each man (except the center) will move in, out or remain stationary, depending upon the particular defensive alignment and the individual's split rules.

Our Basic Split Rules

Our offensive basic split rules are as follows:

EVEN DEFENSE:

1. *Guards*—Full man; don't move.
2. *Tackles*—Man over you, split one-half man. If no one is there, use a common sense split which would be to cut the split down on a wide play and take a maximum split on an inside play.
3. *Ends*—Line up a little over a full man split, and use the common sense split rule which would depend upon the play. Never move more than one-half man either way.

ODD DEFENSE:

1. *Guards*—Take a full man split, but never so wide that if a man should jump into the gap between the guard and center, you could not cut him off. After taking the proper split, then apply the common sense split rule.
2. *Tackles*—If there is no inside linebacker:
    (a) Wide play called—split in one-half man.
    (b) Inside play called—fake split and don't move.
    If there is an inside linebacker:
    (a) Split out one-half man.
3. *Ends*—Take good wide splits and apply common sense rule; never split more than one-half man either way.

In order to split intelligently it is important to determine first of all if the defensive man will move with you when you move (Figure 80a), or whether he is keeping his spacing on his own defensive man

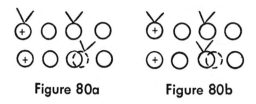

Figure 80a   Figure 80b

(Figure 80b). You must determine as quickly as possible if your defensive man is taking a variable or a static position. Figures 80a-b illustrate variable and static spacing, respectively, by the defensive linemen.

Do not ever emphasize that you are splitting to get good blocking angles, but you split in order to isolate a defender. If the defender splits when the offensive man splits, you can isolate him. If his split is static, a good blocking angle will be the result. Your linemen should never split merely to get the angle, however. It will also help the linemen if they have a clear picture of where the ball crosses the line of scrimmage (the critical point of attack), and from where the ball is being thrown on a pass play. Then, too, there is no set rule that will cover all defensive situations and the offensive men must be able to apply the common sense split rule along with the basic split rule.

Figure 81 illustrates the pre-shift position of the right side of the offensive line and the application of the guard's, tackle's, and end's split rules. From the pre-shift stance and position, the offensive men are allowed to split one-half man either way, according to the defense. The inside always must be protected. A defensive man must not be allowed to penetrate or shoot the inside gap as he would likely stop the offensive play for a loss.

PRE SHIFT	⊕ ◯	◯	◯
GUARD	⊕ ⟨◯◯⟩		
TACKLE	⊕ ◯	⟨◯◯⟩	
ENDS	⊕ ◯	◯	⟨◯◯⟩
LINE	⊕ ⟨◯◯⟩	⟨◯◯⟩	⟨◯◯⟩

Figure 81

136

Our Offensive Running Game

If the defensive man will move with the offensive man, then the offense should be able to isolate one man, and the point of attack. should be directed toward him. Figures 82a-b illustrate the center's man and the offensive right tackle's man being isolated respectively, and the critical point of attack being directed at the isolated defenders.

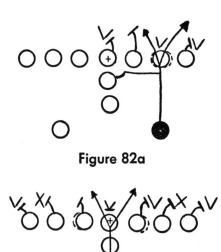

Figure 82a

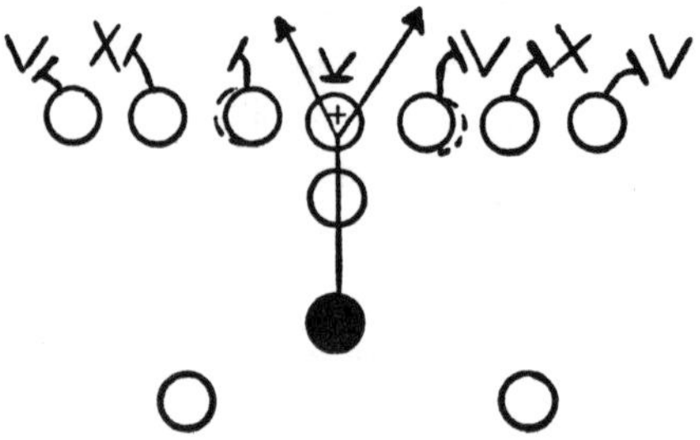

Figure 82b

It is very important for the offensive lineman to know that his main objective in proper line splitting is either (1) to spread the defense out, or (2) to isolate a man. The main objective is never to split in order to get a good blocking angle. This latter misconception can destroy any advantage we gain by splitting the line.

OUR SNAP COUNT

In order for a team to operate at maximum efficiency offensively, all of the players must get off with the ball at the same time. They must uncoil as a unit and strike the opposition as quickly as possible. The only advantage the offense has over the defense is that it knows where the play is going and when the ball will be snapped. In order to maintain this advantage, the offense must strike quickly as a unit. Should the defense penetrate the offense or the offense not get off on the ball together, the offense loses its advantage over the defense.

The offense's advantage hinges on its ability to get off on the ball together. Whether or not the offense can do this well will depend upon their first initial movement, which in turn depends upon the snap count.

At one time or another, I believe we have used just about every imaginable snap count. We have found that our line gets off better as a unit, without leaning, and hits quicker when we employ a sound snap count. The quarterback can say what he likes if we are going on the first sound. While in the huddle, the quarterback will give the play and then cue the action with the first sound, second sound or the third sound. We use the same word for our sound snap count, but the emphasis is placed on the first, second or third sound. For example, if the quarterback calls, "24 on the second sound," the team lines up in its offensive position, and the quarterback says, "Go!" Since this is the first sound, the ball is not centered. Then the quarterback commands, "Go!" for the second sound, the ball is centered and the team moves as a unit. The quarterback can wait between his first and second commands since our snap count is non-rhythmic. Such a measure not only keeps the defense off guard, but it also keeps the offense constantly alert.

Automatics

It is not my purpose to discuss the automatic versus the non-automatic systems of signal calling. In the former, the quarterback can use the automatic system or change the play at the line of scrimmage. In the latter, he runs the play that was called in the huddle and does not change it at the line of scrimmage. There are advantages and disadvantages to both systems. A strong argument that is advanced for the non-automatic system is that it gives the linemen time to analyze their blocks and mentally pick out the persons they are supposed to block as they approach the line of scrimmage. The people who favor the non-automatic system maintain they have fewer broken signals, and fewer bad plays than the teams using the automatic play change.

While I am not stressing the merits of one system over the other, frankly, I would never send my players into a football game without several plays which could be automatic-ed at the line of scrimmage. It is just common sense to realize certain plays are not good against certain defenses, and it is useless in most instances to run a play directly toward the strength of a defense when you need to gain yardage in order to sustain your offensive drive. Therefore, we always have a trap play, an end sweep, and a look pass as our automatics. Since they are few in number, our automatics are easy to learn and they allow the quarterback to change his play at the line of scrimmage if he wishes to do so.

Our automatic system is very simple, and there is very little confusion when we change our plays. As an example, while we are in the huddle, the quarterback will call play, "18," and the players will break from the huddle and go to the line of scrimmage. After the quarterback gets the players down into their offensive positions and he sees he wants to change the play on automatic, he will repeat the original play, "18." This will alert the players, and they know the next number they hear will be the new play that will be run instead of play 18. After the quarterback has repeated the original play, and has called another number, "24," as an example, everyone on the offensive team knows the new play will be 24, and the snap count always remains the same.

Faking the Automatic

If the quarterback wishes to fake an automatic so the opponents cannot catch on to what he is doing, this can be done very simply. As an example, let's say the quarterback called the play, "30," in the huddle. At the line of scrimmage, he decided to fake or dummy the automatic. At the line he will say any number other than the one he called in the huddle. This notifies the players it is a fake automatic and they will not pay any attention to the next number he calls as they are going to run the play which the quarterback called originally in the huddle.

By using this two number system we can always play the automatic or fake it, and it is impossible for the opponents to catch on because they do not know the play the quarterback called in the huddle originally. It is impossible to use the automatic if the quarterback has elected to run the play on the first sound. The majority of the time when we are going on the first sound, we will be hitting fast and straight away, and an automatic will not be necessary. If the quarterback thinks there is any chance he might want to change the play for any particular reason, he would not run the play on the first sound.

THE OFFENSIVE HUDDLE

The entire offensive operation starts with the huddle; therefore, it is very important to insist that proper huddle techniques are carried out properly. It is not too important the way the men are spaced or lined up in forming the huddle, as long as everyone can see, hear and get to their proper offensive positions with as little confusion as possible. It is a must, however, for the quarterback to use the proper techniques in calling his plays and in controlling the huddle.

The Quarterback Controls the Team

A quarterback should never allow any talking in the huddle, unless he asks a question and wants specific information. Therefore, he should stand out of the huddle until it is completely formed. This will give any player an opportunity to come and give specific information to the quarterback without talking in the huddle.

The quarterback should not just call a signal, but on certain occasions he should make a few extra comments while in the huddle. He should be forceful, and above all, he must be confident. The team will run the play the way the quarterback calls it. Occasionally, he should single out the man called on to make the key block and inform him the team is depending upon him. After the quarterback has called the play, and someone wants to check the signal, the quarterback should not merely repeat the signal but the entire play over again.

The quarterback must know the tactical situation at all times. If a substitute comes into the game, the quarterback should always ask if there are any instructions from the coach. The quarterback must always be conscious of the 25 seconds between plays, and he should use it to his advantage, whether to speed up or slow down the game. Training the quarterback will be discussed in greater detail in Chapter 9.

THE QUARTERBACK'S TECHNIQUES

I spoke previously of the quarterback's stance. It is very important for him to take the same stance every time. The center must know where to place the ball every time. Centers and quarterbacks should work with each other frequently giving them as much practice as possible. Each center or quarterback has particular traits, and by the centers and quarterbacks working with each other, they get to know one another better, thus eliminating bad exchanges between them.

The quarterback should have his head up and always look straight ahead, while observing the defense at all times. He should be as comfortable and as relaxed as possible, and he should never look down when receiving the ball from his center.

Taking the Snap-Back

On the snap of the ball, the quarterback should dip his hips so his hands will follow the tail of the center as he charges. This technique will also help the quarterback push off. The quarterback will take the ball with his right hand, using the left as a trapper, as was explained previously. He should make certain he has the ball, and he should not fight it, before withdrawing his hands from the center's crotch. As soon as the quarterback has possession of the ball, he should bring it into his "third hand," his stomach. Such a procedure will help prevent a fumble. He then wants to push off and execute his techniques as quickly as possible.

The quarterback must always be aware of the fact he cannot score without the ball; consequently, he wants to make certain he has possession of it before pulling out of there. If he gets in a big hurry, he is likely to drop the ball to the ground. I have seen this occur many times.

After Receiving the Snap

After receiving the snap, the quarterback will operate in one direction or the other by using a pivot or a crossover step. The theory and techniques are basically the same.

First, the quarterback must know the defensive alignment as this will determine how far he should pivot, or if he needs to take a position step. After he has recognized the defense and he has taken the first short jab step or pivot step, he should have the ball in close to his body until he is ready to hand off.

The head is the first part of the body around if using the pivot step, and also the first to move in the direction the quarterback is taking if the crossover step is used. After the head is pointed in the right direction, the steps can be adjusted to avoid running into the ball carrier. The quarterback should not move his arms or his body up and down as he should maintain the same level throughout the entire operation. The quarterback should never flash (show) the football; he always operates under control.

Making the Exchange

It is important for the quarterback to know each man with whom he must make an exchange, including his speed, strong and weak points. He should look at the target, the far hip, of the man to whom he is going to hand the football, and he should be very quick with the exchange. He should try to make the hand-off with the same motion he would use if he were dealing cards quickly.

Quarterback Faking

The faking of the quarterback is very important. He should always remember to carry out his fakes realistically. Incidentally, we sometimes give the ball to the man who is supposed to be doing the faking. We have found it helps our faking as the man is not certain whether or not the quarterback is going to give the ball to him.

When attempting a fake, it is very important for the quarterback to look at the man he is faking to, and not merely swing his arms in a half-hearted fake. He should go through the same motions he uses when he actually gives the ball to the faker. His fakes must be realistic for the offense to be effective. The quarterback should remember he never stops moving while on offense, except when faking to set up a drop-back pass.

BALL CARRYING TECHNIQUES

Every team wins or loses a great percentage of its games due to the manner in which the backs and ends carry the football. All players, not only the backs, should be drilled in the proper mechanics and techniques of carrying a football properly as it is possible on occasions an interior lineman will have an opportunity to run with the ball.

The outstanding characteristics or strength of each ball carrier are likely to be different as one might possess outstanding speed, another is a nifty, shifty runner, and the third is solid on his feet, possesses power, and is capable of running over the opposition. Every ball carrier must utilize his natural talents, and should practice diligently to become as versatile as possible. Regardless of the individual style of a runner, the most important point is for him to hold onto the football and not fumble it.

Good habits, careful handling, and the execution of proper techniques will prevent fumbles on ball exchanges. When a player has the ball in his possession and fumbles it, he has committed the unpardonable sin in my estimation. The ball carrier should remember to have one point of the football in the palm of his hand with the fingers around the end of the ball, and gripping it tightly. The other end should be in the crook of his arm, which should force the football up close to his body.

If the football is carried properly, and the ball carrier is determined to hang onto it, the football should never be lost due to a fumble. The ball is the most valuable object on the football field. Consequently, if the ball carrier fails to hang onto the ball, he is letting down his entire team. Once a player has control of the ball and fumbles it, this is no accident. It is either carelessness or lack of courage. I can't build a winner with this type of player. In a close game a fumbled ball can be the deciding factor in winning or losing.

A ball carrier should remember his primary objective is to gain ground; if possible, to score. Therefore, he should move directly toward the opposition's goal line as quickly as possible, unless there is a definite reason for doing otherwise. There are always exceptions to the rules, and a ball carrier may not be running toward the opposition's goal because he might be trying to make better use of a blocker, dodge an opponent, get to the opening, time the play properly, or he might have some other valid reason. There will be times when top speed and the correct direction will not be sufficient to get the job done.

Open Field Running Techniques

When a ball carrier is in the open field, he should always keep the tackler guessing. He should not tip off whether he is going to try to outrun him, run through him, or dodge him, until he is close enough to the tackler to give him the fake and then get by him. The ball carrier should never concede he is down, and he should always keep fighting to gain ground until the whistle stops the play.

The ball carrier should always realize and know exactly where he is on the field, and just what he must do in order for the play to be successful. In a majority of cases, a ball carrier should be concerned only with running for a touchdown.

The Importance of Proper Mental Attitude

The basic difference between ordinary and great athletes is mental attitude. As far as football players are concerned, the ordinary ball carrier will try to make a touchdown, but he will be satisfied with a five or six yard gain. The champion athlete, the All-American back, is dissatisfied when he fails to score. He is always going for the opposition's goal line. The ball carrier actually does not succeed in his objective unless he runs for a touchdown on every play (except for occasional tactical situations), and he should never be made to feel he has accomplished his objective unless he scores.

A ball carrier must be made to realize that when he does a poor job of carrying the ball the effort of the other ten men has been wasted. The ball carrier must always be aware of the yardage necessary for a first down and for a touchdown. When the ball carrier has possession of the football, he must realize he has the control of the game in his hands.

OUR BLOCKING TECHNIQUES

Blocking techniques are basically the same for all linemen. The blocks the backs are called upon to execute are basically the same, too. Therefore, we will not discuss the techniques of each position, but merely discuss techniques and procedures as a whole.

The Drive Block

The drive block or the one-on-one block was developed primarily for a fast-hitting attack, and is one that we use on many occasions. All blocks consist of the following steps: (1) the approach, (2) the contact, and (3) the follow-through.

APPROACH:

1. Approach with short, controlled steps. First step should be with the outside foot, and it should not go beyond the forward foot. The knees should be bent at this time.

2. Split the opponent's course with the first step, and aim the nose guard at the middle of the opponent's target.

3. Keep the eyes on the target at all times.

4. Uncoil off the forward foot. Do not duck the head during the uncoil.

CONTACT

1. Strike a jarring blow with the shoulder.

2. Bring the head up as contact is made, sliding head to one side on contact. (The body will follow the head; this will help arch the back.)

3. The drive should be forward, then upward. The object is to knock the opponent off balance, thus depriving him of his traction; this will make him easy to move out of the play.

4. Bring the feet up fast with short, choppy, digging steps, but still keeping the knees bent.

FOLLOW-THROUGH:

1. Stay on feet with the knees still bent and keep driving.

2. Keep the feet well spread and under the body.

3. Charge through the opponent.

4. Keep the body between the opponent and the path of the ball carrier.

The most important single step in the drive block is keeping the feet driving the instant contact is made.

The Reverse Shoulder Block

This block is used primarily when the blocker already has position on a hard charging lineman.

APPROACH:

1. Aim the far shoulder for the opponent's far hip. This will help allow for the opponent's charge.

2. Shoot the head and shoulders in front of the defensive man.

3. This movement must be sharp and on a straight line.

4. Take a short positive step with the inside foot.

CONTACT:

1. Uncoil off the near foot.

2. Strike a good blow on the opponent's hip, squeezing with the neck and head in the stomach.

3. Bring inside foot up to help cut off penetration.

FOLLOW-THROUGH:

1. Bring the legs up fast and keep them driving.

2. The charge of the defensive man will put the blocker in a perfect blocking position.

3. Keep the body weight into opponent.

4. If and when the opponent attempts to spin out, go into a crab position around the outside thigh to prevent pursuit.

Blocking Linebackers

The percentage of time the offense can block the linebackers will determine to a great extent how successful the offense will be. If the linebackers are blocked, the defense will usually break down.

APPROACH:

1. Get off on snap of the ball.

2. Whenever possible, release to the inside to block an inside linebacker; to the outside when blocking an outside linebacker.

3. Stay low, don't run in a circle, but take the shortest route to the linebacker.

4. Get to the point of attack in position to block before the linebacker can get there to defend it.

5. Keep your body between the linebacker and the ball carrier.

CONTACT:

1. Split the linebacker right down the middle with initial block.

2. Thrust the body forward and upward, hit the linebacker on the rise and elevate the shoulders on contact.

3. Strike the blow with a low fundamental position, hit with shoulder and forearm, sliding head to one side on contact.

4. Make contact, keeping feet underneath the blocker, and maintaining a wide base. It is impossible for the blocker to follow through properly if he lunges or leaves his feet before or while making contact.

FOLLOW-THROUGH:

1. As soon as contact is made with the linebacker, continue the leg drive. The initial blow should knock him off balance and the leg drive should keep him this way.

2. Keep the weight into the linebacker.

3. Gain position follow-through. The blocker should continue to strive for position to eliminate any possibility of the linebacker being in on the tackle downfield.

Downfield Blocking

The approach of the downfield block will vary with the play called and position of the defensive secondary men. The approach we will discuss will be centered around attacking the defensive halfback.

The downfield block is a definite characteristic of all good football teams, and it is virtually impossible to have many long runs without good downfield blocking.

APPROACH:

1. Release rapidly on the line of scrimmage.

2. Sprint shallowly just beyond the line of scrimmage.

3. When approaching the designated person to block, aim for a spot in front of his original position; this eliminates running behind the halfback when he comes up to make the tackle.

4. The blocker must have a clear concept of the point of attack and the prescribed path of the ball carrier.

5. The blocker should make the defensive man commit himself before he starts to make contact.

CONTACT:

1. Once the defensive man has committed himself in a specific direction, the blocker then starts his contact.

2. The blocker will get as close as possible to the defensive man (about two yards) execute a high drive block. He will maintain his block as long as possible, thus allowing the ball carrier who breaks into the open field to use the blocker to make his cut.

FOLLOW-THROUGH:

1. The follow-through will consist of maintaining contact as long as possible and using the defender's momentum to take him where he wants to go. The ball carrier can break off the blocker's position.

The Post-Lead Block

The post-lead block, or two-on-one block, is used to insure the blocking of the most dangerous defensive man, and at the same time, give the ball carrier the feeling of confidence that he can concentrate his efforts on whipping the one defensive man to the inside or outside of the man being double-teamed. With this in mind, the blockers are more conscious of turning the defensive man away from the play rather than driving him straight down the field. By using this same method, it makes it possible to cut off the pursuit.

APPROACH:

(Post Man)

1. Drive straight at the defensive man with short controlled steps. First step is with the outside foot.

2. Aim the nose guard at the middle of the target.

3. Keep the eye on the target at all times.

4. Uncoil off the forward foot.

(Drive Man)

1. Take a position step with the inside foot and then a good step with the outside foot to get squared away.

2. From this new position, aim the nose guard at the middle of the opponent and use as an apex. From this position, the middle of the opponent would be below the armpit and just above the waist.

3. Keep eyes on target all the way.

CONTACT:

(Post Man)

1. Strike a good blow with the forearm and shoulders.

2. Drive straight through the opponent to stop his charge.

3. Hit on the rise and keep the pressure applied, keeping the knees bent at all times.

(Drive Man)

1. Strike a jarring blow with the shoulder below the armpit of the opponent.

2. After good contact, slide head past body and continue applied pressure with the inside shoulder.

3. Keep the tail down, head up, and feet under the body.

FOLLOW-THROUGH:

(Post Man)

1. After good contact and feet are well up under the body, turn the tail toward the drive man.

2. Keep pressure applied, feet moving in short, choppy steps, and drive man down the line.

(Drive Man)

1. Keep pressure with shoulder and neck, and do not let man spin out to outside.

2. Keep the tail to inside and do not allow defensive man to split.

3. Keep feet moving in short, choppy steps and move man down the line.

4. Force defensive man into pursuit to help eliminate it.

The Trap Block

APPROACH:

1. It is important to take the same stance as if going straight ahead, but just before the ball is snapped, the weight is shifted to the outside foot.

2. Take a quick, short, 6-inch step with inside foot and point toe directly toward spot to be trapped.

3. Never raise the body up. Stay down and in a semi-coiled position.

4. Drive off the forward foot, still taking short steps.

5. Anticipate the person to be trapped, to be filling the inside or floating in the hole.

CONTACT: (see below)

FOLLOW-THROUGH:

The contact and follow through are exactly the same as on our drive block, which I explained previously.

The Pass Protection (Drop-Back Pass)

This technique is used by the guards and tackles when protecting the passer on a straight drop-back pass. It is good to go from a pre-shift position when using this type of block.

APPROACH:

1. Take a short step backward with the inside foot, then a longer step backward with the other foot.
2. While doing this, turn the tail slightly to the inside and remember the inside gap must be protected.
3. After the second step backward, the blocker should be in a good position (tail down, head up, knees bent, back straight, and the body in a cocked position ready to strike a blow).

CONTACT:

1. Look at the man to be blocked, make him come to the blocker. When close enough, spring and attack him, trying to make contact with him at the numbers.
2. After contact is made and the charge of the offensive man has been stopped, the blocker will take a step back, regain his football position and make contact again.
3. At all times, the blocker will be forcing the defensive man to the outside.

FOLLOW-THROUGH:

1. When the blocker sees that the defensive man is taking a definite side in his charge, the blocker will slide his head in front and drive him in the direction of his charge.
2. At all times the blocker will maintain contact and work his feet around to force the defensive man to the outside, thus keeping him away from the passer.

The Crackback Block

This block is used primarily by the ends when they are blocking an inside linebacker. It can also be used by anyone who might be blocking directly in front of the ball carrier.

APPROACH:

1. Release from line of scrimmage as quickly as possible.
2. Aim block into the numbers of the linebacker.
3. Get within a yard and a half before going into block.

CONTACT:

1. Execute high drive block.
2. Maintain block as long as possible.

FOLLOW-THROUGH:

1. Stay on feet with the knees still bent and keep driving.
2. Keep the feet well spread and under the body.
3. Charge through the linebacker.
4. Keep the body between the linebacker and the path of the ball carrier.

The most important single step in the drive block is keeping the feet driving the instant contact is made.

The Junction Block

This block is used primarily by the fullback when he is blocking a true end or a corner man on a wide play.

APPROACH:

1. Aim for a spot about a yard in front and outside of man to be blocked.
2. Run low and hard at spot.

CONTACT:

1. Extend the head and shoulders in front of and past the defensive man. (The blocker's head is pointing downfield.)
2. The blocker will use his inside leg and hip to catch the outside leg and hip of the defensive man.

3. The blocker will drive his head and shoulders past the defensive man with his inside leg firmly against the outside leg of the defensive man, and with his hands down and his tail up.

FOLLOW-THROUGH:

1. Force defensive man to go inside by keeping feet moving and driving downfield.
2. Do not extend body and fall flat on the ground.
3. Do not let man spin to blocker's outside.
4. Keep pressure on defensive man as long as possible.

The Arc Block

This block is used when a small back, in particular, is trying to block a true end or corner man on the ground.

APPROACH:

1. Hips open to sideline.
2. Turn upfield and aim for outside hip of contain man.

CONTACT:

1. Slip head past the defender.
2. Contact is made with inside shoulder at hip level.

FOLLOW-THROUGH:

1. Keep feet moving.
2. If block is not held, roll into defender.

NUMBERING THE DEFENSIVE ALIGNMENTS

In making our blocking rules or assignments for all of the players versus all different defensive alignments, there are several factors to take into consideration. The rules must be simple, and second, they must be brief. We have used several different kinds of rules, such as, "Inside gap, over, linebacker," and others. This was a good method, but it amounted to quite a bit of memory work for the players because the majority of the blocks were all different sequences. Trying to adhere to the theory, "the simpler, the better," we started numbering the defensive men as illustrated in Figure 83a versus the 5-4 defense alignment; 83b versus the wide tackle 6; 83c versus the gap 8 defense; and Figure 83d versus the Eagle defense.

We start counting with the man over the center and number him zero, and from there go both left and right numbering every

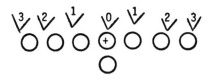

Figure 83a

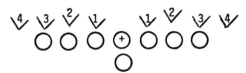

Figure 83b

Figure 83c

Figure 83d

man within two yards of the line of scrimmage, as illustrated in Figures 83a-b-c-d. We also number the men in the secondary. We do this by merely continuing with our numbering beyond the end lineman in the direction the ball is going to go, as illustrated in Figure 84a versus the Oklahoma 5-4 defense, and Figure 84b versus the wide tackle 6-2 defensive alignment.

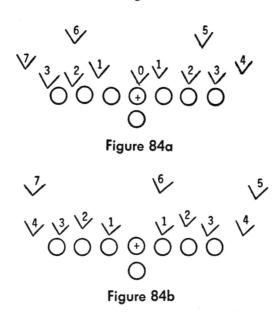

Figure 84a

Figure 84b

ATTACKING THE DEFENSIVE ALIGNMENT

Probably, like many other football teams, we have too much offense. However, in order to do an intelligent job of planning our attack versus the numerous defensive alignments, one must have sufficient offense since not all plays are good against all defenses.

Regardless of one's offense, the first approach is to establish a good sound middle attack that is based on the trap, fullback handoff, and a pass off the same action. Unless a team can force the defense to respect the inside power and force the defensive linebackers and guards to stay "at home," it is almost an impossibility to perfect the outside attack. After we establish the inside attack, we want to run far enough inside the defensive end to cut down his quick containment. The next step, then, is to perfect the wide attack and the corner passes, in order to have a well-rounded offense. Bootleg passes, reverses, and an occasional trick play are also needed in order to keep the defense "honest," and to make the above-mentioned plays more effective.

GOING WIDE

It is an offensive must for a team to be able to go wide and to get the long gainer. Occasionally, all of us get a good gainer from the inside attack, but most long gainers are from passes or some form of wide attack.

Previously we operated on the assumption that if we could gain four yards on each play we would score with a sustained drive. Statistics will prove a team will generally stop itself by some error, or the defense will stop the offense, before the attack can make four consecutive first downs or gain 50 yards, a majority of the time. Consequently, a team must perfect its wide game.

There are several ways of going wide, but regardless of the manner attempted, the defensive end or corner man must be eliminated either by blocking him, optioning him, or throwing the football over his area.

Wishbone Attack

The wishbone attack is built around a hard-running fullback and a quarterback who can read defenses and run. There are several "musts" in personnel if this attack is to be successful. First of all, the fullback must be able to explode at the tail of the guard and not let one man tackle him. Second, the halfback must be able to run wide and also perform the junction block, and third, the quarterback must be able to make a fast decision on whether to give the ball to the fullback, keep it himself, or pitch it to the offback. We must establish a strong inside running game, but we are constantly trying to get the ball outside. The wishbone alignment is illustrated in Figure 85.

Inside Veer Right

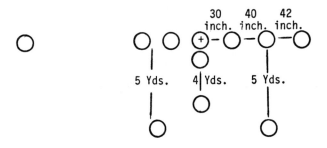

Figure 85

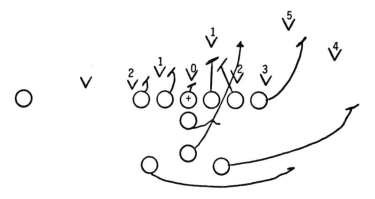

Figure 86

There are several basic wishbone plays that must be mastered, as follows:

> On End— #5.
> On Tackle—First inside linebacker; N/T, gap.
> On Guard— #1.
> Center—Over, gap, off-side.
> Off Guard— #1.
> Off Tackle— #2.
> Near Back— #4.
> Fullback—Veer route.
> Off Back—Pitch.
> Quarterback—Read #2, Option #3.

COACHING POINTS:

    1. Fullback explode at outside foot of guard and expect the ball.

    2. Quarterback must read #2. (If he stays outside, give fullback the ball.)

    3. Both halfbacks must explode laterally.

Inside Veer Left

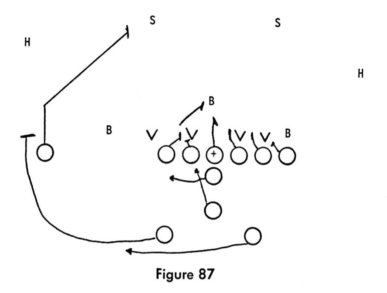

Figure 87

On End—Read secondary; get force.
On Tackle—Inside linebacker; N/T, gap.
On Guard— #1.
Center—Over, gap, off-side.
Off Guard— #1.
Off Tackle— #2.
Off End— #3.
Near Back—Read and block force man.
Fullback—Veer route.
Quarterback—Read #2 and option #3.
Off Back—Expect pitch.

COACHING POINTS:

1. Fullback explode at outside foot of guard and expect the ball.

2. Quarterback read #2.

3. Both backs explode laterally.

Outside Veer Right

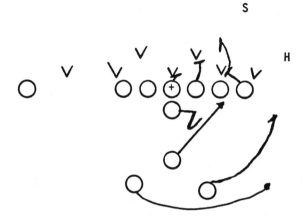

Figure 88

On End—First man to inside, slip to linebacker.

On Tackle— #2.

On Guard— #1.

Center—On gap, over, off gap.

Off Guard— #1

Off Tackle— #2.

Near Back—Junction block containment.

Fullback—Wide veer route.

Off Back—Expect pitch.

Quarterback—Read #3 and option #4.

COACHING POINTS:

1. Fullback does not expect ball; help on #2.

2. Quarterback think keeping the ball.

Outside Veer Left

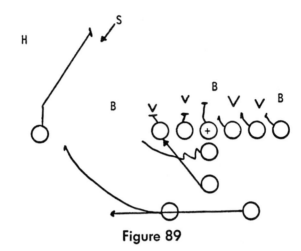

Figure 89

On End—Read secondary; get force man.
On Tackle— #2.
On Guard— #1.
Center—On gap, over, off gap.
Off Guard— #1.
Off Tackle— #2.
Off End— #3.
Fullback—Outside veer route.
Near Back—Junction block.
Off Back—Pitch.
Quarterback—Read #3 and option #4.

COACHING POINTS:

1. Fullback does not expect the ball.
2. Quarterback "think" keeping the ball.

Power Sweep Right

On End— #3.
On Tackle— #2.
On Guard— #1.
Center—On gap, over, off gap.

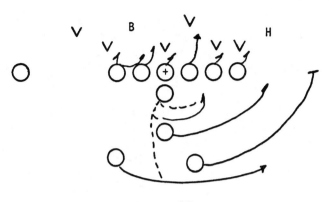

Figure 90

Off Guard— #1.
Off Tackle— #2.
Fullback— #3; If 3 blocked, go to safety.
Near Back— #4.
Off Back—Carry ball.
Quarterback—Reverse out and pitch.

COACHING POINTS:

1. Quarterback, after pitching, look back to inside for tackle or guard who might be coming down the line.

Power Sweep Left

On End—Halfback.
On Tackle— #3.
On Guard— #2.
Center—On gap, over.
Off Guard— #1.
Off Tackle— #2.
Off End—Safety.
Near Back— #4.
Fullback— #3.
Off Back—Ball carrier.
Quarterback—Reverse out and pitch.

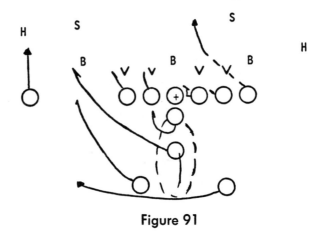

Figure 91

COACHING POINTS:

1. After quarterback pitch, look quick to inside for escaping guard or tackle.

Blast Right or Left (only toward tight end)

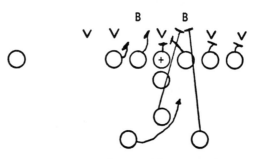

Figure 92

On End— #3 out.
On Tackle— #2 out.
On Guard— #1; N/T, inside.
Center—On gap, head on, off-side.
Off Guard— #1.
Off Tackle— #2.
Fullback—First inside linebacker; N/T, middle linebacker.
Near Back—First inside linebacker; check #2.
Off Back—Ball carrier.

COACHING POINTS:

1. Alert to check off if no linebacker.

These are the basic plays of the wishbone, as illustrated in Figures 86, 87, 88, 89, 90, 91, and 92. There are many, many more plays with counters, cross plays, reverses, and different kinds of options, but these plays are what will make it go. Without these plays, you have no wishbone attack.

It is also a must that you be able to break your wishbone and put people in motion, split out your backs as well as your tight end.

CONCLUSION

My objective has been to present each phase of our offensive running game which can be utilized against the various defensive alignments. My philosophy is to keep the offense simple, be sound in our coaching, and never settle for anything less than perfection in its execution.

CHAPTER 8

Our Offensive Passing Game Techniques

THE PASSING GAME IS ONE OF THE TWO MAIN WEAPONS of offensive football. In order for your passing game to be successful, you must sell this phase of football to your players, and then have good protection, good receivers, and a good passer. These essentials of a good passing game go hand-in-hand, and no combination of any two is any value without the third.

THE PASSER

It is beyond the wildest expectation of any optimist to hope for a good passing game without a good passer. Therefore, select an individual who has the natural ability to throw. There are certain things one can and cannot teach a passer.

It was my good fortune to have Joe Namath, one of the finest natural passers in modern-day football. Since his motion was natural, we coached him very little, other than on the basic mechanics of grip, holding the ball, etc. I feel it is possible to over-coach the passers, the same as the kickers.

The Grip

Assuming a player has natural throwing ability, the first coaching point to teach is the grip. It is generally preferred for the passer to grip the ball with the point of his little finger touching almost in the center of the lace. We feel if the points of any of his other fingers touch the lace, he will be gripping the ball in the center (the roundest part of the football), consequently limiting his ability to get a good grip on it. A passer definitely cannot throw the ball properly if he grips it with the point of the forefinger, middle or third finger touching the lace. The grip is very important. The passer should not grip the ball as tightly in bad weather as he ordinarily does under more ideal playing conditions.

When employing the wishbone, the quarterback is required to fake with the football, and then set up to pass. Therefore, he must always bring the football back into his stomach after every fake. When the quarterback's forearms are touching his hips in a relaxed position, he is able to keep the football closer to his body and it is easier to hide. During the faking of the ball, the quarterback should shift his entire weight toward the back, rather than toward the extension of the arms and the extended football. This, too, is very helpful to aid in hiding the football after the faking is completed.

The quarterback should be ready to throw the football the instant he gets back and sets up. The ball should be held with both hands until the passer is ready to release it or fake a release. This procedure will insure the passer's being in a relaxed position, which is vitally important. After the passer has set up to throw the ball, it should be in a cocked position at his ear. This position enables the passer to save time as he prepares to release the football.

The Release and Delivery

Releasing and delivering the football are next. If the passer has learned the grip and how to hold the football as explained above, then the release and delivery will come more easily. The passer must release the ball with a snap of the wrist. Very few passers have a good, natural wrist snap. Consequently, there are few good natural passers. The wrist snap can be developed by drills, and we use several different types.

In delivering the football, which is actually part of the release, the passer, except in rare instances, should step toward the intended receiver as he throws the football. Not only will the passer be more accurate, but he will be going in the correct direction to cover his pass in case of an interception, when he steps and throws in the same direction. If he steps in one direction and attempts to throw in another or attempts to throw across his body, the passer is throwing from an awkward position and throwing against his own weight.

The Footwork

Perfecting the passer's footwork is very important. He must know the spot from which he is going to throw the ball prior to his actual passing. It is especially important for the protecting line and backs to know the spot from which the passer is going to throw. They cannot do an intelligent job of protecting him unless they know, and unless he makes certain he actually throws from that spot. When throwing from the pocket, the passer must retreat straight back, set up as quickly as possible, and stay inside the pocket formed by his linemen and remaining backs.

The running or optional pass is one of the best passes in modern-day football. It should be perfected by those teams that base their attack partially on wide plays. There are no definite rules or steps for the passer on the running pass, because all athletes are a little different. What might be right and proper for one passer on his fifth and sixth steps would be wrong and improper for another passer due to individual differences. Nevertheless, the passer should have the ball up and in a position ready to throw it by the time he reaches a spot directly behind the area where his offensive end lined up originally. He should start upfield as quickly as possible. This not only makes the play more effective, but it also puts him in a position to run if the defensive man drops back to cover the pass.

Individual Passing Principles and Techniques.

Passing is one phase of football in particular that needs constant practice and close attention. It is also one phase which is overlooked and underworked by teams that do not have natural passers. The following individual principles and coaching points should prove helpful in teaching a player with natural throwing ability how to be a better passer:

1. Push off with the left foot (right-handed passer).
2. Hide the ball on the way back to set up.
3. Set up quickly.
4. Get at least seven yards deep on most drop-back passes.
5. Be under control when you set up, and be sure to be in a good position to throw the football.
6. Look straight downfield.

7. Stay in your pocket while throwing.
8. Keep the arm cocked, and the ball high at all times.
9. Step in the direction of your pass.
10. Throw the ball out-of-bounds if no receiver is open.
11. Know the pass routes.
12. Know the receivers.
13. Know the weak and the strong defenders.
14. Know when to drive the ball or pull the string on it.
15. Don't throw interceptions.

PASS ROUTES

A good passing game is based on the following primary objectives:

1. To flood an area, that is, to have more receivers in a particular area than there are defenders.

2. To get a one-on-one situation, and .et the offensive man outmaneuver the defensive man by using various cuts or patterns.

Flooding an Area

Flooding an area is perhaps the easiest and surest way of having a receiver open or in a position to catch the ball. The basic thinking in this particular type of passing game is to assign two or three receivers to a particular area, as illustrated in Figures 93-95, making it impossible for one or even two defenders to cover the receivers if they stay spread out and run their routes properly.

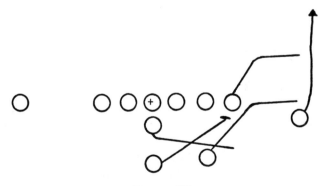

Figure 93

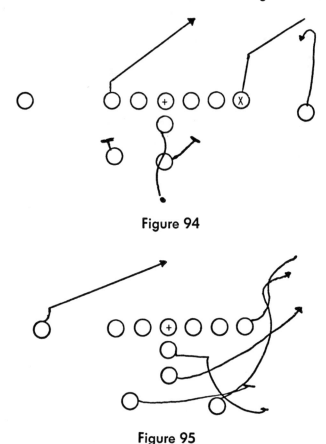

Figure 94

Figure 95

Offensive Pass Cuts

There are numerous offensive sets a team can employ in order to force the opposition to use man-on-man coverage. When using different sets and formations, I think it is more advisable to teach all of the eligible receivers pass cuts, rather than having them classified under pass patterns which would affect the whole team. As an example, the quarterback could call a formation that would set the left halfback right and split the left end out. He could then call a pass pattern to his right which would be a pattern to flood a particular zone, and at the same time call a particular cut for the left end who will try to outmaneuver the defensive right halfback—who might be forced to cover him alone. Figures 96-99 illustrate several individual pass cuts, such as, sideline, deep, out, drive, circle, stop, Z-in and Z-out.

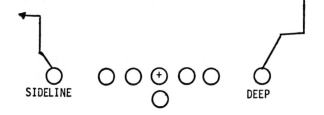

SIDELINE   DEEP

Figure 96

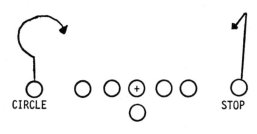

CIRCLE   STOP

Figure 97

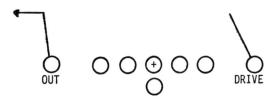

OUT   DRIVE

Figure 98

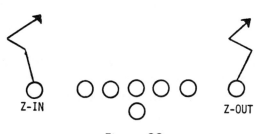

Z-IN   Z-OUT

Figure 99

PASS RECEIVING

A football team can have a great passer and good cuts and patterns, but unless the receivers do their jobs correctly the passing game is of little value. The pass receiving phase is broken down into the following six basic maneuvers: (1) the release, (2) the approach, (3) faking, (4) running, (5) catching the ball, and (6) running with the ball.

Release:

To be a good and consistent receiver, the first prerequisite is clearing the line of scrimmage. A good receiver should never be held up at the line of scrimmage. He must work on this important phase of the passing game in order to perfect it. Every time an end releases downfield on running plays, he should experiment on techniques which will aid him later on pass plays. No two defenders are the same. What is successful against one might not be successful against another defender.

Approach (Man-for-man coverage):

Straight Line Approach:
1. Run at three-fourths speed.
2. Run at a specific point of the defender's body.
3. Force the defender back, attempting to get him to turn in the opposite direction of your final break.
4. Make a good fake and step in the opposite direction of your final break.

Weave Approach:

1. Run at three-fourths speed.
2. Run an irregular course.
3. Through the change of direction, force the defender to change his feet.
4. The number of weaves made will be determined by the cuts called and the depth in which the ball is to be caught.
5. Give the impression that each weave is to be the final cut.

Faking (types):

1. Head fake—accompanied by a short jab step in the opposite direction of the final break.
2. Roll step—fake one way and roll off back foot directly toward the defender.
3. Change of direction.
4. Hook.
5. Hook and go.

Run (immediately after faking to receive the ball):

1. Run under control and relaxed.
2. By running three-fourths speed, the receiver is able to adjust to poorly thrown balls.
3. Keep the arm action parallel to the leg action until ready to catch the ball.
4. While running, turn only the neck and head. If the body is turned at the waist, the receiver will be slowed down considerably.

Catching the Ball:

1. Relax completely as the ball comes toward you. Relax particularly the fingers.
2. Follow the ball with the eyes all the way into the hands.
3. Catch the ball in and with the hands.
4. Never attempt to trap the ball next to the body.
5. Eliminate all thought from the mind except catching the football. All great receivers concentrate to such a degree they are actually unaware of the presence of the defenders.
6. A ball thrown directly at chest level or higher should be caught with the thumbs in. If the ball is thrown below the chest level, the thumbs should be turned out.
7. Always try to get the body in front of the ball on short passes.
8. A ball thrown on the outside and away from the receiver should be caught with the thumbs out.
9. When attempting to catch a long pass, never allow the inside arm to be in a position to blind you from seeing the football.

10. Catch the ball and tuck it away before running with it.

11. Every pass thrown to a receiver belongs to him, and he should exert every effort to catch it.

12. If the receiver cannot possibly catch the football, he should not permit the opponent to catch it. This is a cardinal rule.

Running (after catching the ball):

1. As soon as the ball is caught, take it firmly in the hand, tuck it under the arm, and most important, do not fumble.

2. Drop the inside shoulder expecting immediate contact.

3. Turn upfield to score.

CONCLUSION

Offense is based on two primary principles, running with and/or passing the football. The passing and running games supplement and complement each other. Neither phase is of particular value, however, unless the quarterback knows when, where, why and how to use each phase, along with the kicking game. Training the quarterback will be discussed in Chapter 9.

CHAPTER 9

Training the Quarterback

ALL OUTSTANDING FOOTBALL TEAMS HAVE TWO DISTINCT CHARAC-
TERISTICS IN COMMON—a great fighting spirit and a great quarterback.
A smart, capable quarterback is the greatest single asset a football
team can possess. Success in a football game is determined mainly
by the selection of plays. Poor selection of plays will destroy team
morale and nullify the finest of teamwork.

Quarterback generalship is simply the application of good
common sense. It consists of two parts—knowing what to do and
making the team do it. If a team has confidence in its quarterback, it
is likely the plays selected will be successful. If a team does not
have confidence in its quarterback, it is likely the plays will not be
successful. The "right" quarterback inspires confidence. One manner in which the quarterback builds confidence is through the selection of proper plays. I do not mean to imply the "right" quarterback
can grab-bag any play and make it work. If he is wrong frequently
as the result of his grab-bag selection of plays, his teammates will
lose confidence in him. If we have too many bad plays, we call them
from the sidelines.

THREE TYPES OF QUARTERBACKS

There are basically three types of quarterbacks. There is the
quarterback who makes positive mistakes, due to his total disregard
for the basic principles of generalship. He does not know his offense, and has little understanding and knowledge of why his plays

are not effective. He is unaware of what the defense is doing. Generally he calls plays quickly—any play to get the team out of the huddle. He destroys team morale and spirit. His team generally loses badly. He is not coachable. I cannot build a winner with this type of quarterback, and I consider him highly undesirable.

The quarterback who works to avoid mistakes is a second type of individual. He does what he is told and taught, but from a tactical and mechanical standpoint only. Generally he lacks initiative. He tends to be conservative in his quarterbacking. His errors and mistakes are not the glaring, positive type, as in the first case cited. Although he is not brilliant in his quarterbacking, he is dependable.

The third type of quarterback is the one every coach is seeking. He directs his team to maximum results. He is a student of the game. He is logical in his thinking, and bold in his action when it is necessary to win the football game. He is confident, which in turn gives his team confidence in him and the offense. He is a winner through preparation, and he will give you winners through his action and leadership. Unfortunately there are few such quarterbacks of this type. Consequently, you must take what you have and develop what you've got. Regardless, however, a good quarterback must be a natural leader, be smart, have initiative and resourcefulness, be unselfish, have a good voice, and good mechanical ability. If your quarterback lacks the ability to inspire your team to do its best on every play, it is not likely you will have a winner.

From time to time, I have been blessed with smart quarterbacks—and we have had winners then. I attribute much of this success to my backfield coaches who have spent considerable time with the quarterbacks teaching them the what, when, why, and how of offensive football, and a knowledge of defensive football so they can do an intelligent job of field generalship. As I indicated previously, without proper play selection, it is almost impossible to win the tough football games.

FIELD POSITION

Of the many factors that go into selecting a play, probably the most important single factor is field position. To aid our quarterback in his play selection, we divide the field into different areas and zones, as illustrated in Figure 100. Each zone is given a name, and there are some very important "musts" concerning each area.

We divide the field into the following areas and zones, with the most important coaching points listed as follows:

The "Must Zone (Goal Line to 3-yard Line)

In this zone, we must move the ball out at least to the 3-yard line so it will be possible to kick from spread formation. Our kicker stands back 13 yards deep when we kick from our spread kick formation.

The Three-Down Zone (3-Yard Line to 25-Yard Line)

1. We must make a first down with three plays.
2. We do not like to punt while in this zone. If we can hold the football until we get past the 25-yard line, we can put the opposition in their three-down zone with a 40-yard kick.
3. Run trap plays.
4. Anticipate a short yardage defense occasionally.

The First Down Zone (25-Yard Line to 40-Yard Line)

We must make a first down so we can continue to control the ball when we reach the Free Wheeling Zone.

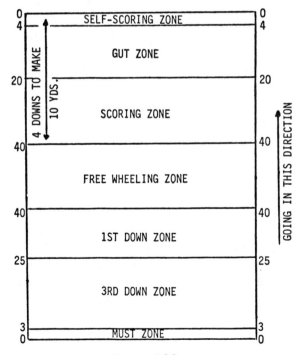

Figure 100

The Free Wheeling Zone (40-Yard Line to 40-Yard Line)

1. Easiest part of the field to score from.

2. Go into our game planned offense.

3. It is a guessing game until you make a good gain, so you should be a play ahead of the defense. Once you gain this advantage, keep the pressure on the defense.

The Scoring Zone (40-Yard Line to 20-Yard Line)

1. Try to score with a trick play or a scoring play which you have set up.

2. You may use a play the scouting report indicates should work.

3. Figure on four downs to make the 10 yards.

The Gut Zone (20-Yard Line to 4-Yard Line)

1. Must "out gut" them.

2. Do not lose ground.

3. Try to get five yards or more on first down.

4. Pass on first down or waste down.

5. Must maintain control of the football.

The Self-Scoring Zone (4-Yard Line to Goal Line)

1. Minimum handling of the football.

2. Score yourself if you have a play per yard.

3. Do not pull linemen.

4. Throw the ball from play action.

5. Give the football to the best ball carrier.

6. Must score.

Our Three MUSTS:

Our quarterback must continuously remind our team of three very important principles affecting our offense, which are as follows:

1. We must not get a penalty.

2. We must not break an offensive signal.

3. We must get our men (blocks).

After your quarterback is thoroughly familiar with the zones and their relationship to each other, then you can do an intelligent job of instructing and teaching him which plays should be run in the various zones. Consequently, he will have a better understanding of field position.

RECOGNIZING AND ATTACKING DEFENSES

When working with our quarterbacks "picking" a defense, we never tell them to attack the opposition's weakness but merely to run away from their strength. The only time your quarterback really needs to know how to recognize a defense and its strengths and weaknesses is when he is changing plays at the line of scrimmage. Otherwise your quarterback will call specific plays in certain zones or areas according to your scouting report and game plans.

There are two basic defensive alignments, which are even and odd. If there are defensive men playing over our guards, we call this an even defense. If there are no defensive men playing over our offensive guards, we call this an odd defense.

With respect to the secondary, there are two alignments. They are 3-deep and box. If there is a safety man, it is a 3-deep secondary and an 8-man defensive front. If there is no safety man, it is a box defense and there are nine men in close proximity to the line of scrimmage, or a 9-man front.

Recognizing and Attacking an 8-Man Front

After the quarterback has determined whether the defense is odd or even, and the secondary is 3-deep or box, he should then look and determine the number of men who are playing outside of his offensive end. By doing this he can determine if the strength of the defense is inside or outside. If there are two or more men outside of his offensive end, as illustrated in Figure 101, the strength of the defense is wide. Consequently, the quarterback should run inside plays, away from the strength of the defense. As illustrated in Figure 101, by looking through the inside and outside lanes it is easy to see that these defenses are fundamentally the same.

You can definitely run against an 8-man front, as illustrated in Figure 101, because by splitting properly the defense has only two men outside of the offensive ends. Consequently, you can run wide. Or the defense must have four men or less inside your end, in which event you can run inside with your basic offensive attack.

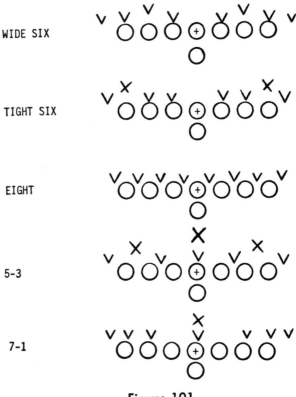

WIDE SIX

TIGHT SIX

EIGHT

5-3

7-1

Figure 101

The defensive team playing a gap 8 defense, as illustrated in Figure 102, is trying to get penetration by shooting the gaps. The quarterback must recognize what the opposition is attempting to do, and he must eliminate the bad play. Consequently, he should work slightly off the line of scrimmage in order to avoid being tackled before he can hand off. The strength of the defense is inside. Consequently, the quarterback must run the corners. The game situation and field position will determine which play the quarterback will call. The quarterback should never throw a counter pass or a back-up pass versus the gap 8 defense because all the defenders cannot be blocked. He stands a better chance of scoring if he selects a corner pass. The block or action pass is very good because it helps to eliminate the bad play.

Figure 102

Recognizing and Attacking a 9-Man Front

If it is not a 3-deep secondary, then it is a 9-man front. All 9-man fronts are basically the same, as I have illustrated in Figure 103.

The quarterback wants to run at the man who is isolated in the defense, and in most cases it is the defensive man over the offensive center's area. The attack can go wide, too, but the offensive team must do an intelligent job of splitting in order to draw the defense in tight. If the offensive guards take wide splits and the defensive men move out with them, the defensive man over the center will be isolated and the quarterback can direct his attack toward the middle.

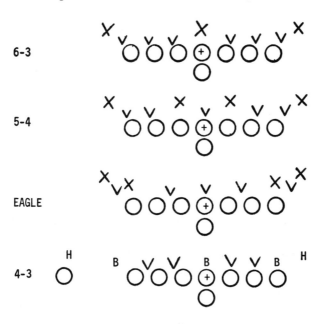

Figure 103

The corner passes versus a 9-man front, with the quarterback exercising his option of running or passing, are excellent because of the pressure exerted on the corner man. If he drops off to cover an area for the pass, the quarterback must run with the football. If he rushes to contain the passer, the short flat is open for a pass.

It is very important to teach your quarterbacks the different defenses, and the strength of each defensive alignment. As I mentioned previously, we teach the quarterbacks to run away from the strength of the various alignments. The quarterback must also be aware of the fact that he does not have to whip the entire defense, but only the weak area in the defense. If a defensive man is isolated or if there is no defensive man on the line in a particular area, we consider this the weak part of a defensive alignment.

Playing the Game on a Blackboard

We have a number of meetings with our quarterbacks going over strategy and game situations and drilling them in the principles of quarterbacking and field generalship. It is difficult to expect a quarterback to make the correct decision at a critical time in a game unless he has been drilled to react to such a situation. With this in mind, for years I have used the procedure of having our quarterback coach and the quarterbacks play a game of football on the blackboard.

In order to explain our procedure more clearly, let's assume it is early September and we are preparing for our opening game with the University of Georgia. We have been drilling our quarterbacks daily on the defenses we expect Georgia to use in various parts of the field. We have been drilling them on how to attack these particular defenses with our offense. With this basic information, we are now ready to work with the quarterbacks at the blackboard playing our football game.

A coach goes to the blackboard and draws a diagram of a football field, along with the defenses we expect Georgia to use on the hashmark, in the middle of the field, on the goal line, and in a short yardage situation. On the board, the coach will also list the backfield personnel, so the quarterback will have an opportunity to use his men properly. To digress for a second: the quarterback uses the wrong judgment if he calls for sweeps with a slow backfield, does not employ the best blocker to block, etc. The quarterback must know his offensive personnel thoroughly.

The coach then explains to the quarterbacks, who are observing what he is writing on the blackboard, the condition of the field, wind, and the other tactical factors. It is now time to play the game with a particular quarterback.

The coach will select a quarterback and say, for example, "Georgia kicked-off to us and we returned the ball to the 25-yard line on the right hashmark." The coach will plot the position on the diagram. The quarterback will then take into consideration the defensive alignment we expect Georgia to employ in this particular section of the field, and the quarterback must call a play accordingly. If he makes what the coach considers a good call, the coach will say, "You made four yards on the play. It is now second and six." If the quarterback makes a bad call, the coach will say, "You lost three yards on the play," and he will explain why the call was a poor one. If the quarterback takes too long in calling his play, he receives a five-yard penalty. When the quarterback makes a very good call, the coach gives him a long gain or a touchdown.

By using this game, a quarterback can learn to call plays by anticipating defenses in areas all over the football field. He also learns to use his personnel properly. We have found this game at the blackboard has helped our quarterbacks tremendously.

While one quarterback is playing the game, the other quarterbacks are listening. If the quarterback at the board fails to make a first down, he must punt, and the coach appoints another quarterback to take over. After each play the coach will plot the position of the ball on the diagram, and the players learn to know which defenses to expect. We have found, with other things being equal, that the quarterback who has the mental ability to sustain the ball for a long drive and a touchdown will usually be your best quarterback.

We also spend quite a bit of time going over situations. The coach will cite a specific situation, and then say, "What would you do in this situation?" The situations are usually the clutch ones, and should the quarterback select the wrong answer in the game it is likely to lose the contest. Even though you drill the quarterbacks, there is no fool-proof method of making certain they will always make the right decision. The following example will illustrate my point.

Early in September, a few years ago, our backfield coach, Phil Cutchin, was going over situations with our quarterbacks and said, "We are playing the University of Houston (our second game). We are ahead by six points. There are five minutes remaining to play. We are on our own 18-yard line. It is a first-and-10 situation, and Houston is playing a 5-4 defense. What would you do?" One quarterback said quickly, "Coach, I would throw a corner pass into the sideline." Phil answered, "Yes, and they would intercept the pass, return it for a touchdown, kick the extra point, and we would lose the game, 7-6." The quarterback saw his mistake and said he was glad we had gone over this particular situation.

Three weeks later the same quarterback was faced with almost the identical situation, except that we were ahead by three points. The other factors were the same as previously cited. What did the quarterback do? He threw the corner pass into the sideline, and Houston intercepted it. Fortunately Houston did not score! The point I am trying to make is your quarterbacks will still make mistakes even after you have worked with them.

THE QUARTERBACK'S GUIDE

In order for a quarterback to be outstanding, he must be cognizant of certain pertinent information relating to his offense, the opposition's defense, tactical and strategical information, and the principles of quarterbacking and field generalship.

Offensive, Defensive and Tactical Information

The following information is of value and significance to the quarterback:

Information a Quarterback Must Know About His Own Offense:

1. Know your teammates thoroughly, including your best ball carrier, your best blocker, best pass receiver, best faker, etc.

2. Know all of your plays and everyone's blocking assignments.

3. Know where every receiver is on every pass pattern.

4. Know your best play and pass against every defense.

5. Know and understand how each play fits into a series.

     6. Know and remember the plays that are working—keep running them.

     7. Know the reasons for the proper line splits.

     8. Know the plays the players have the most confidence in.

     9. Know the best plays for special situations—draw, screen, etc.

    10. Know how to stop the clock.

Information a Quarterback Must Know About the Defense:

     1. What defense are they playing?

     2. Who is making the tackles?

     3. Are they stunting their defenses?

     4. What type of pass coverage do they use?

     5. Do the linebackers run through?

     6. Are the ends crashing?

     7. Who is tackling the passer?

     8. Who is the best defensive man?

     9. Which man can we isolate?

    10. How quickly does the secondary revolve?

Information a Quarterback Must Know About the Game:

     1. Time left to play is a big factor.

     2. Timeouts left.

     3. Weather and field condition.

     4. Know which down it is at all times.

     5. Field position.

     6. What yard line the ball is on.

     7. Which zone the ball is in.

Game Strategy

     The following game strategy information is of value and significance to the quarterback:

General Information:

     1. Always know score, time to play, yards to go and down.

     2. Know your field zones, and avoid giving the ball to the opposition in the 4-down zone.

     3. You are playing for a victory, but remember a tie is better than a defeat.

     4. Know your own personnel and each man's capabilities.

5. Know all there is to know about your opponents by studying scouting reports and movies.

6. Know your offense, including the blocking assignments.

7. Be able to recognize any defensive alignment.

8. Understand the importance of field position.

9. Know when not to pass.

10. Know when to kick.

11. Use the wind intelligently.

12. Know when not to try for a score.

When to Kick

1. When in doubt.

2. Kick early with a strong wind or against a weak offense. From 40 to 40-yard line, kick straight away and high. Inside 40-yard line, kick out of bounds.

3. When score is even, or you are ahead, always make safe kick to 3-down zone.

4. Kick early on a wet field; let the opponents handle the ball.

When Not to Pass:

1. When the opponent expects a pass.

2. When you have two downs to make six yards or less.

3. In your own territory, just before half time.

4. When backed up and you are ahead.

Type of Pass Throw:

1. On long yardage, throw short passes or to third man out. Draws, screens.

2. On first down, play passes.

3. On waste downs, play passes, long passes, and screens.

4. When time is short, throw near sideline.

5. When in doubt, throw optional passes.

On Wet Field:

1. Play conservatively.

2. No difficult ball handling.

3. Avoid bad places on field, also wide plays and cut backs.

4. Do not be afraid to pass.

When Not to Try For Score:
1. Just before half time, behind your own 40-yard line.
2. When you are running clock out.
3. When you are preparing to give a safety.
4. When you have one down to make first down—go for first down.

When To Try to Score In One Play:
1. When you have mental edge on opponent following a blocked kick, a recovered fumble, or an intercepted pass in the opponent's territory.
2. Just before half time in the opponent's territory.
3. On waste down in opponent's territory.

When To Run Your Best Ball Carrier Behind Best Blockers:
1. When you must have a first down.
2. In four-down zone going in for a score.
3. Clutch down in danger zone, coming out.
4. Save your best ball carrier in the free wheeling zone.
5. Do not use him first play after a long run.

What To Do On Clutch Down:
1. Fake and give.
2. Some kind of an optional play.
3. Best ball carrier behind best blocker.
4. Waste man effectively.
5. When trying to save time, tell ball carrier to go out of bounds.

Scoring Area:
1. Waste man effectively.
2. Best ball carrier behind strongest blockers.
3. First down inside three—run ball yourself. No ball handling.
4. Make sure that on fourth down you will have the ball in the middle of the field where you can try any type of a scoring play.

What To Run On Waste Down:
1. Safe, long gainers.
2. Fake-give, or optionals are normally effective.

When To Speed Up Offense:
1. When you are behind.
2. Inside the opponent's 15-yard line.
3. When you have the wind to your back.

When To Slow Down Your Offense:
1. When you are trying to kill time.
2. Just before the half in your own territory and you are ahead.
3. Fourth quarter, if more than one touchdown ahead.
4. When the wind is against you.

Free Wheeling Zone:
1. Try for long gainer.
2. Use sideline intelligently.
3. Use wind intelligently.
4. Use best ball carrier as decoy.
5. Utilize various formations.
6. Try long gainer on first down and second down and go for first down on third down.
7. Call trick plays that have been set up earlier.
8. Try to keep ball in middle of field.

Quarterback Must Remember:
1. Poor field position calls for conservative plays.
2. When you are ahead and the game is drawing to a close, play slowly, conservatively, and very deliberately.
3. When you are behind and the game is drawing to a close, play faster, be more reckless, and get the ball out of bounds to stop the clock.
4. When you are in scoring territory, you must score. Any yardage gained without scoring is of slight value only.
5. Any yardage you make deep in your own territory which does not serve to get the team into the free wheeling zone is of slight value.
6. If you are ahead by 11 points and there is not more than five minutes remaining to play and there is a strong wind against you, it is smart to take a safety instead of trying to punt out from inside your 10-yard line.
7. Time works with you when you are ahead; against you when your team is behind in score.

8. Figure what the defense would normally expect in any given situation, and then do the opposite.

9. If a play fails, you must know why.

Tips For Quarterbacks:

1. You must have genuine confidence in yourself and your ability.

2. You must have the confidence and respect of your team.

3. You must have personality and leadership; then exercise it.

4. You must know the ability of your own personnel.

5. Play the percentages for ultimate team victory. Consequently, you must study scouting reports and have a clear picture of the game plan. You must be able to recognize defenses immediately, and be able to direct your attack away from the strength of the defense. You should think with the defensive signal caller by putting yourself in his place. Remember it is a guessing game until you make a gain. After a gain you should be one play ahead of the defense.

6. Eliminate bad plays as they will defeat you. Any play that does not gain is a bad play. Only a fumble or a penalty can stop the offense if you eliminate the bad plays.

7. Run more offensive plays by getting out of the huddle quickly.

8. After a penalty or a time out, have your play called and the team ready to play at the line of scrimmage. Do not follow this procedure when trying to run out the clock.

9. Try to score in one play after a break in an effort to demoralize the defense. Should you follow this procedure several times and not be successful, discontinue it; otherwise, you will demoralize your own team.

10. Never try to score just before the half from deep in your own territory. Run out the clock and get a fresh start the second half.

11. When you are behind, never try to score in one play. Play the game as if it were a tie contest; otherwise, you can be out of the game before you realize it.

12. Normally we like to pass on first down and on a waste down. On short yardage, throw play passes. On long yardage, throw in front of the deep men.

13. First down is your important call. If you make five yards or more, you have the advantage. If you fail to make four yards, the defense has the advantage.

14. On clutch downs and short yardage, run fake gives because the defense must go to the first fake under such circumstances.

15. Remind your line to tighten up on the goal line, and do not call plays that require linemen to pull as the defense may break through and throw us for a loss.

16. Do not pull a play out of the hat. If you are in doubt, run an option run-pass.

17. We will rehearse weekly every situation possible, such as saving time, killing time, giving up a safety, sideline offense, etc., so that you will automatically make the right decisions in the game.

CONCLUSION

It is virtually impossible for a quarterback to know and do everything correctly. However, a coach must work with his quarterback, and the individual must spend many additional hours studying and preparing himself so he will be able to handle any situation that arises. It is an absolute must for your quarterback to be well prepared if you expect to have a successful football team. If you are rebuilding a football team, it is very important for you to pick your quarterback first, find out what he can do well, and then build your offense around him.

CHAPTER 10

Planning for a Game

PₗₐₙₙᵢₙG FOR ANY PHASE OF FOOTBALL IS IMPORTANT, but planning for a particular game is vitally important. I tell my players our staff will study, prepare and plan one hour for every minute the players are on the practice field. Then we actually spend this much time in our practice and game preparation. The typical fan has little conception of the amount of time we spend planning for a single football game.

OUT-OF-SEASON PLANNING

Our planning commences in early summer when I assign each assistant coach to a particular game opponent for the coming season. If we do not have as many coaches as we have football games, several assistants will have to double up and prepare for two opponents.

Each coach will secure as many movies as possible on his particular opponent and break down the films. He also familiarizes himself with the returning personnel, and studies each player's characteristics, strengths and weaknesses. The coach will observe the returning quarterback's movements in particular, looking for tip-offs. Does he look at his receiver all the way downfield? Does he have a favorite pass route? Does he have a favorite receiver? Does he favor action or drop-back passes? Does he like to operate to his left or right? Such information, along with additional scouting information, helps us get a "book" on the quarterback.

It is important to know the opposition's strongest and weakest positions on offense and defense. The coach looks at the films, and attempts to get as much reliable and valid information as possible from them. Then when the coach (scout) sees his opposition in the fall, he will do a better job of scouting them because he is familiar with the offense, defense, and the returning personnel.

IN-SEASON PLANNING

During the season, we like to see an opponent play at least three times. We feel we can do a better job of planning after we have a fairly clear understanding of what our opponents are likely to do. We want to have a fairly definite idea of what our opposition will do offensively in the following situations:

1. First down and 10 yards to go.
2. Second down and long yardage.
3. Second down and short yardage.
4. Third down and long yardage.
5. Third down and short yardage.
6. Fourth down and short yardage.
7. Unusual and special situations.

Conversely, we want to find out what our opposition will do defensively versus the above situations.

In order to give you a run-down of our procedures, let's consider a typical week preceding Saturday's game.

Sunday's Schedule

The coaching staff will meet together early Sunday morning and go over the film of Saturday's game. While the assistant coaches are studying and grading the film, I will meet with the assistant coach who scouted the team we will be playing this coming Saturday. In addition to receiving a thorough scouting report from him, I want his recommendations, offensively and defensively, of what we should do against the opponent. The scout will then complete his report as he will present it to the squad members on Monday night.

In the meantime, the other assistant coaches have completed their grading of the film, and then we discuss personnel. As the result of game performance, we commence to make plans as to the personnel we will be using in the upcoming game.

Monday's Schedule

On Monday morning, the scout will give his report to our entire staff. He then answers questions relating to the opponent we will be playing on Saturday. After we have fully discussed the opposition from every aspect, our defensive coaches will have a separate meeting and make plans to set up the defenses which they would like to use. The offensive coaches have a similar meeting, and map out their strategy versus all of the various defenses the opposition has used in various situations. We recognize the fact that some plays are good only against certain defenses and not all plays are successful against all defenses. Therefore, we try to limit our offense to the best possible plays against our opposition's anticipated defenses. Of course, we must have a valid, reliable, comprehensive scouting report in order to make our plans. We also understand and recognize the fact that some teams will change practically their entire offensive system from game to game. However, this gives such teams only one week to perfect a new "favorite" series, and this is almost an impossible feat.

All of our coaches will meet together again around 10:30 A.M., with the defensive coaches making their recommendations for Saturday's opponent. The strategy is discussed at length before a decision is reached. Let me digress for just a second to say that once we have made our decisions, we will stick with them for fear of confusing our players by changing defenses later in the week.

The procedure is repeated again, this time with the offensive coaches. All coaches, regardless of position or whether they specialize in offense or defense, will enter the discussion. We have found following such a procedure helps us do a better job of coaching, and some of our best suggestions relating to offense have come from our defensive coaches, and vice versa, defensive suggestions have come from the offensive coaches. We are always open to suggestions!

After we have made our plans, we can then make out our work

schedule for Monday afternoon. Although I usually make out the remainder of the schedule for the week each night after practice, you can see the necessity of waiting until Monday in order to make out the day's work schedule.

After lunch, we will have a short squad meeting. First, we go over last Saturday's game discussing both the good and bad points. Then we will inform the squad of our plans for this coming Saturday's game, and change assignments, make adjustments, etc., at this time.

The players who do not have late afternoon classes meet at 3:30 P.M., and we go over last week's game movie. Each coach will sit with the players whom he has graded and discuss their performance in the film. If time permits, we like to have the ends and backs meet in one group and the interior linemen in another group for separate viewings of the film. We feel such a practice is highly desirable and eliminates the confusion that generally occurs when all of the players view the game film at the same time.

On Monday and Friday our regular practice commences at 5:30 P.M., since our men take their laboratory classes on these two days. It is impossible to set up a practice schedule if key personnel are absent due to late labs every day of the week.

The players who played in Saturday's game will be out in sweat clothes for approximately 45-50 minutes. They will stretch and loosen up, before we spend most of the time learning and rehearsing the defenses they will be using for this coming Saturday's opponent. Our procedure is to have the "red shirts" come out of the huddle and line up in the different offensive formations we expect to face, and our defense will adjust accordingly. For the last 15 minutes of the session a scrub team will run the opposition's favorite plays about half-speed so the regulars will have an opportunity to familiarize themselves with the offense. Then the players in sweat clothes take several short sprints and we send them to the showers.

The players who did not play in last Saturday's game have a good workout emphasizing and practicing fundamentals. At times we terminate Monday's practice session with a short scrimmage against the freshman squad.

After a late dinner on Monday night, we have another squad meeting where the scout will give a complete oral report to the players on our upcoming opponent. He will discuss personnel, favorite plays, passes, defenses, kicking game, and any additional pertinent information relating to the opposition. He then hands out a comprehensive typed scout report to the squad members. Frankly, I do not believe a player can do an intelligent job of playing without studying his scouting report.

Tuesday's Schedule

We will have a staff meeting early on Tuesday morning in order to set up the practice schedule for the afternoon. A typical Tuesday practice session will last approximately one hour and 35 minutes, plus the last period which does not have a specific time limit for the reasons I explained previously.

Our schedule is generally set up so that the first five minutes the linemen will be firing out and hitting the big sled or seven dummies, and the backs will be having a fumble drill or working on stance and starts. Our exercises and agility drills precede this drill for the linemen and backs.

The second period will usually be 20 minutes in duration, which will vary from week to week according to our needs. A typical period will have our first team secondary working on pass defense against a scrub team that will be throwing the opponent's passes. At the same time, in another area we will have our first and second team guards and tackles working on defensive techniques. Our backs will be divided into two groups. One group will work on our polish drill, and the other on the secondary drill. Our third and fourth lines will be working as teams on blocking.

At the termination of the previously mentioned 20-minute period, we exchange the backs and linemen, and the coaches repeat the drills again with their new groups.

Our next period will be working on individual techniques by positions for approximately 15 minutes' duration. During this time, our coaches generally work on weaknesses or correct errors which they observed in last Saturday's game film. Or they will work by positions on recommendations which were made at Monday's coaches' meeting.

Our team drills and "team learning" are next on Tuesday's practice schedule. The first and third teams will work on our offense for Saturday's game. The first team will run about three plays to one compared to the third team. During this time, the second team will work on defense against the scrub team, which will be running the opposition's plays and passes. At the termination of 20-25 minutes, the first and second teams will change around, with the first team working on defense, and the second and third teams working on offense. This period continues for 20-25 minutes.

The first and second teams will work on the kicking game next. As I stated previously, we use our kicking game as a conditioner and at the same time do something functional with respect to perfecting our protection and coverage. When they do it properly, normally this phase of the practice schedule lasts 10-12 minutes. If not executed to our satisfaction, the period is longer in duration. While the first two units are working on their kicking game, the third team will usually be working on their defensive play. After completing their 20 minutes' defensive drill, they must have their kicking game practice.

After we have set up Tuesday afternoon's schedule, we will amend offensive and defensive plans if necessary. We generally spend the remainder of Tuesday morning evaluating player personnel.

After lunch we will have a short squad meeting for about 15-20 minutes if we have amended our offensive or defensive plans or if we are going to make any changes of any nature involving the offense or defense.

Some time after lunch and before our specialists take the field at 3:10, with our regular scheduled practice commencing at 3:30 P.M., our defensive coach will meet with our defensive signal callers and our offensive coach will meet with our quarterbacks, and go over defensive and offensive plans and strategy, respectively.

After practice we will have a brief staff meeting again and we will review our entire practice schedule. At this time, I want my assistant coaches to make recommendations for the next day as I want to work on the schedule at night for the following day. I discussed our procedures in Chapter 3.

Wednesday's Schedule

The procedure is the same as previously—staff meeting and set up the afternoon's practice schedule, which will be about one hour and thirty minutes, excluding the last drill which is not timed.

After setting up the exercises and the agility drills, we will have our linemen firing out, the same as on Tuesday, and the backs will be polishing plays.

The next 25-minute period will be first team on defense against the scrub team, and they will practice defense over the field. The scrub team will run the opposition's plays and tendencies, and the defense is full speed with the exception of tackling the ball carrier. During this time, on another field our second and third teams will be running our offense versus the opposition's defense.

During the next period the first and second teams will exchange and repeat the same drills listed above.

The next period will usually be 20 minutes' duration with the third team working on defense over the field, and the first and second teams working on special situations such as quick kicks, passes, etc.

The next period will be devoted to our kicking game. We also usually have a few goal line drives on Wednesday.

Our Wednesday's practice schedule will vary more than the other days because we spend about 20 minutes on group drills and about six minutes full speed on goal line defense, and phases of this nature.

After Wednesday's schedule is completed and out of the way, the staff will usually go to the projection room and view films of this week's opponent.

After lunch we will again have a short meeting and inform the squad of any changes we have made or plan on making. We will also discuss the previous day's practice.

The defense signal callers and the quarterbacks will meet separately with their respective coaches for about 20 minutes, which is our usual procedure daily during the football season.

After Wednesday evening's dinner, we have a squad meeting and go over the film of the opponent we will be playing on Saturday.

Thursday's Schedule

Thursday morning we will again have an early staff meeting and we set up the afternoon practice schedule first.

After five minutes of firing out for the linemen as units, and the backs working on stance and starts or a quick fumble drill, we will have three 25-minute periods where we will stress learning and perfection more than body contact.

We will have three different groups working at the same time. The first unit will be working on offense versus the opposition's defenses, over the field. The second unit will be working on their defenses versus the opposition's offense, being run by the scrubs over the field. The purpose of this is to check our defensive signal caller to see that he is calling the correct defense in various sections of the field. In a third area we will have the third team working on all phases of the kicking game, such as quick kicks, spread punt, punt returns, on-side kick, etc.

At the termination of the 25-minute period, the teams will change. The first unit will go to the defensive drill; the second unit to the kicking drill; and the third unit will go to offense.

When the second 25-minute period has terminated, we will change for the third period. Following such a procedure gives each unit 25 minutes of offense, of defense, and on the kicking game. Then we send the players to the showers because we do not want them to leave their game on the practice field and be tired on Saturday.

After Thursday's schedule is set, the staff will spend the remainder of the morning discussing the progress which has been made to date in preparation for our forthcoming opponent. We also discuss personnel at this time.

After lunch we will have a very short meeting, merely taking time to discuss or review our defensive game plans. Our defensive signal callers and quarterbacks will meet as usual, as I mentioned previously. Our regular practice session will commence at 3:30 P.M.

The coaches meet after practice, as is our usual procedure. We do not meet with the squad on Thursday evening after dinner, however.

Friday's Schedule

Since Friday's practice schedule will not be longer than 30 minutes' duration, we do not have to spend much time in setting it up. We will work as a group and have a short, snappy workout in sweat clothes, going over all of the situations that are likely to occur during the game. After we rehearse kick-offs, returns, on-side kicks, and a couple of goal line drives, we send the players in. As I stated previously, due to Friday afternoon labs, our practice session will commence at 5:30 P.M.

A typical Friday evening dinner menu, if we are playing on Saturday afternoon, would be as follows:

> Tomato soup
> Fruit cocktail cup
> 14-ounce choice sirloin strip, medium well-done
> One-half baked potato mashed, topped with American cheese
> Green beans
> Assorted bread (but no hard French bread)
> One pint of milk or iced tea
> Vanilla ice cream, one dip.

After dinner we will go to a movie as a group or we go some place where we will be together. At 10 P.M. the team will return from the movie to the dormitory or hotel where they are staying. Lights will go out and players will be in bed by 10:20 P.M. the night before a game.

Saturday's Schedule

On Saturday morning the football managers will telephone the players in their rooms at 8:30 A.M. The players who want coffee or juice will be served at 9 A.M. The pre-game meal will be served at 10 A.M., and will consist of the following:

> 11-12-ounce choice surloin strip, well-done
> Green peas
> Dry toast, two slices (no butter)
> Honey
> Hot tea (no cream).

We will have a squad meeting at 10:30 A.M., and leave for the stadium at 12:10 P.M., preparing to meet our opposition at 2 P.M. During the squad meeting we will go over all tricky situations that might arise during the game. After the meeting the defensive and offensive coaches will meet with the signal callers and quarterbacks respectively, and review our final game plans.

After we arrive at the stadium, we send our passers out to warm up about 31 minutes before game time, and the backs and ends will come out about 26 minutes before game time. Our linemen start warming up about 30 minutes before the game. As 2 P.M. approaches, we always feel we are ready and we have done the very best we can to get ready for our particular opponent.

I failed to mention a procedure we follow which we think is highly desirable. During the week of the game, the assistant coach who scouted Saturday's opponent lives in the football dormitory with the players. From 7:30-10:00 P.M. nightly, when we do not have squad meetings, he will show films of the opposition in the dormitory. He will answer questions and give the players any information they are seeking on our opposition. We find our players do a better job when they understand why we ask them to do something. On the field many times we do not have the time to explain why. The assistant in the dormitory does have the time to explain why and as a result the players do a more intelligent and better job of playing.

GRADING THE GAME FILM

Grading the game film is a very definite part of our planning. If we do not know who is doing what during a game, we can't do an intelligent job of planning and coaching. I am sold on our grading system, and we feel that through the study of films we can determine whom to play, and also whom not to play, in critical situations. Knowing this information in advance has won a number of football games for us.

Our procedure for grading films is for one coach to take one position and grade every player in that position offensively and defensively. It is possible for a player to get one of three possible scores, plus (+), minus (−), or ungradable (U), on each play. Our criteria are as follows:

Plus (+)—If the player carries out his assignment and gets his job done properly, his coach will give him a plus. His technique of execution might not be the way he was taught, but we are concerned with the fact that either he did or did not do his job.

Minus (−)—If the player failed to carry out his assignment and/or his man "whipped" him, then he is graded minus (for the particular play).

Ungradable (U)—If a player is not shown in the picture or he does not have the opportunity to help out on the play, he is ungradable and would receive (U). An example would be the defensive right end when the play goes away from him and in all probability he will not have an opportunity to take part in the play.

After getting a grade for each play, like symbols are added together, and the total number of offensive (or defensive) plays participated in to determine percentages. Divide the sum total of plus and minus signs into the total number of plus signs in order to arrive at the percentage of plays that got the job done. We have found that a player must grade at least 61 percent on offense and on defense in order to be a winning football player.

We grade the offense and defense separately. If a player consistently makes a good grade on defense and a poor grade on offense, we know either we have to play him only on defense or we must give him more offensive work.

We have several other expressions, which we have borrowed from baseball terminology, that we use in our grading system. They are as follows:

RBI—Stands for runs batted in, and means something extra good, such as intercepting a pass, causing or recovering a fumble, blocking a punt, throwing a key block—a real clutch play. These are what we call the "big plays" and they are the ones that win the tough games for you. We place a great deal of emphasis on the big play. Frankly, we would rather have a player make three or four RBI's, even though his grade is only 50-55 percent, rather than a player get 65-68 percent and never make any big plays.

Errors—If a player busts an assignment, gets a penalty, misses a tackle in the open field, permits a receiver to get behind him, fumbles the ball, or commits some act of a similar negative nature, we consider this bad and he is given an error. A player who consistently makes two or three errors per game simply cannot play for us. His play will cost you more ball games than you will ever win with him. Consequently, we watch the errors column very closely when we are grading film.

CONCLUSION

Coaching football is a race against time. Time lost on the practice field can never be regained. We attempt to utilize every minute possible in preparing for our opponents and our practice sessions.

CHAPTER 11

Our Drills

THERE ARE MANY GOOD FOOTBALL DRILLS. Since we place a great deal of emphasis on defensive football, it is only natural that our drills for the most part emphasize individual and team defensive techniques.

DRILLS FOR THE SECONDARY

The following drills are used to teach individual and team techniques for the defensive secondary:

Defensive Cuts Drill (6-8 men)

With a defensive man standing in a good football position, the coach will move the ball back and forth, and the player will plant, pivot to the inside and sprint in the direction the coach is pointing the football. He will then throw the football and the defensive man will sprint to catch it. The Defensive Cuts Drill is illustrated in Figure 104.

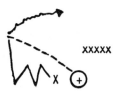

Figure 104

Intercept Drill (8-10 men)

Eight or 10 secondary men will line up behind each other. One player at a time will run toward the coach who will throw the football directly at the player, or to either side of him. The defensive man should intercept the pass, as illustrated in Figure 105.

Figure 105

Tip Drill (8-10 men)

Following the same lineup and procedure described previously for the Intercept Drill, instead of the player catching the football he tips it back to another player who is trailing him, who intercepts the pass. The Tip Drill is illustrated in Figure 106.

Figure 106

Running the Line Drill (6-8 men)

A defensive man will line up straddling a line about 35 yards long, facing the coach. On a command from the coach, the player will start backward using a crossover step, but keeping his eyes and head on the coach. He will try to change direction as many times as possible, always using a crossover step, keeping his eye on the coach (passer), as he zigzags properly from one side to the other down the 35-yard line. (Running the Line Drill is not illustrated by diagram.)

Covering Third-and-Fourths Drill
(2 complete defensive secondaries)

The entire secondary can be set up in a 4-spoke or 5-spoke defense, as illustrated in Figure 107. A coach, simulating a passer, will stand facing the unit. He will simulate either an action pass or a drop-back pass, and the men must react properly to the simulated backfield action. When the ball is thrown, all defenders must sprint for it. The ball is placed on either hashmark and in the middle of the field, and a full offensive backfield may or may not be used to establish flow for the defensive secondary's proper reaction.

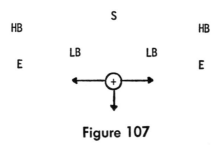

Figure 107

Dog Fight Drill (for defensive halfbacks and corner man) (6-8 men)

Place a defensive halfback or corner man in his regular position. A pass receiver runs a direct route in front of the defensive man's regular position. A coach or passer throws the ball, and we want the defender to play full speed through the receiver for the football, as illustrated in Figure 108. It is merely one-on-one and gives both the receiver and defender practice fighting for the ball.

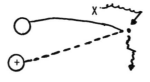

Figure 108

Dog Fight Drill for Safety Man (8 men)

We put a safety man in the middle of the field and receivers on each hashmark. On a signal from the coach, the receivers start down the field and the passer drops back with the football. The safety man must stay in the middle of the field as he gets depth in order to be in a position to cover both receivers. When the ball is thrown, the safety man sprints full speed for the interception, as illustrated in Figure 109.

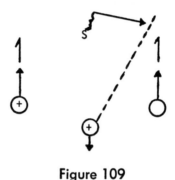

Figure 109

Outside Drill (15-25 men)

We set up a skeleton offensive unit of ends, center and a complete backfield versus the defensive ends and secondary, as illustrated in Figure 110. The offense works full speed running its outside plays and passes, and the defense is drilled in stopping the wide attack.

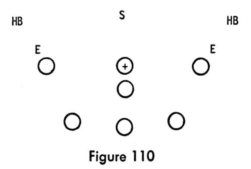

Figure 110

Big Tip Drill (2 complete secondaries)

The entire defensive perimeter is used in our Big Tip Drill, illustrated in Figure 111. A coach will establish flow by running to his left or right simulating backfield action, and the defense must react and rotate accordingly. The coach will then pass the ball, simulating an action pass, and the defender nearest to intercept the ball will yell an oral signal indicating he is going to tip it. The other defenders get in a good football position, and look for the tip. As the first man tips the ball, the defender nearest to it will intercept it and return the pass. The others will head downfield as blockers.

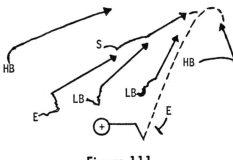

Figure 111

Tackling Drill in the Secondary (8-10 men)

Figure 112 illustrates a drill which we use on the sideline, teaching our backs to utilize the sideline properly as the "twelfth man." The dots represent shirts which are placed six yards from the sideline. The defensive tackler (T) gets in a good football position, which I have described previously, and makes the ball carrier come to him. The ball carrier may take any course or use any individual tactic he wishes to evade the tackler, as long as he stays inside the six-yard area. We do not want the tackler to meet the ball carrier head on, but we want him to approach his man from an angle, keeping leverage on the ball carrier in order to force him out of bounds. The tackler should keep his head in front of the ball carrier, and should try to butt the football with his helmet.

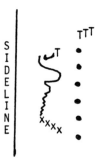

Figure 112

DRILLS FOR THE DEFENSIVE ENDS

The following drills are used to teach individual and team techniques for the defensive ends:

Peel-Off Drill (10-12 men)

Figure 113 illustrates a good drill to teach reaction and to protect his area, which we use for our defensive ends. The end assumes his normal defensive position. The first backfield blocker attempts to block the end, then the second, and finally the third blocker. As soon as the first man leaves, the second starts, and then the third blocker leaves, giving the defensive end experience in playing one blocker at a time but in rapid succession.

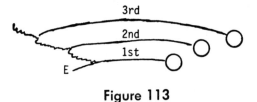

Figure 113

"Reading" Drills (8-12 men)

Figure 114 illustrates a "Reading" Drill which we use for our defensive ends. The end has to play properly the block of the offensive end, pulling guard, on-side halfback and/or the fullback. These are the situations he will face in a game. This drill teaches quick reaction and play recognition for the defensive ends.

All Secondary Drills

Since we consider our ends as part of our defensive secondary, as I explained previously, they will take part in all of the drills explained and illustrated in Figures 104-112, if feasible.

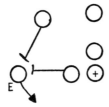

Figure 114

DRILLS FOR THE DEFENSIVE INTERIOR LINEMEN

The following drills are used to teach individual and team techniques to the interior linemen:

Butt Ball Drill (8-10 men)

An offensive man is given a football and told to run a straight line laterally back and forth, carrying the ball on the side he is moving toward. The defensive man must be in a good football position moving back and forth with the offensive man, butting the football with his forehead. He bounces back and forth and keeps butting the football, trying to knock it out of the ball carrier's arm. The tackler's head should be up and his back straight. (The Butt Ball Drill is not illustrated by diagram.)

4-on-1 Drill (6-8 men)

Figure 115 illustrates four offensive blockers playing one defensive man. The coach stands behind the defensive player, and indicates by hand signal the starting count and the blocking assignments of the offensive men. The defensive man must react to the various blocks—double-team, wedge, trap, etc., and fights pressure.

COACH

Figure 115

A & M Wave Drill (9-12 men)

On a signal, the offensive men will uncoil on the defensive men, as illustrated in Figure 116. The defenders must control the blockers with their hands and forearms, locate the ball and pursue in the direction the coach points or runs with the football.

COACH

Figure 116

3-on-3 Drill (16-24 men)

The offense runs a hand-off to the right or left halfback, or to the fullback. The coach, standing behind the defensive team, indicates which back will carry the football. The defensive man varies his techniques from head on, inside, outside or linebacker. If the play is in one defensive man's area, he must whip his blocker and make the play. The other two defenders take proper pursuit angles on the ball carrier. The drill is full speed both ways, and we do not want the men stopping until they hear a whistle. Figure 117 illustrates our alignment for the 3-on-3 Drill.

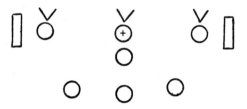

Figure 117

Middle Drill (14-25 men)

The middle drill is similar to the previous drill, only the interior linemen are used offensively and defensively, as illustrated in Figure 118. The defensive alignments are changed around and the offense runs all situations. At times, we use the down marker and chains simulating down and distance when doing this drill.

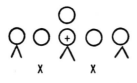

Figure 118

7-Man Spin-Out Drill (8-12 men)

Figure 119 illustrates a player moving from a good defensive position hitting the sled, spinning out, and hitting every other pad on the machine. If moving to the right, we want the players to hit the sled with the right shoulder, keep a tight arc, spin out correctly, and deliver a good blow to the alternate pad. We drill the players right and left as we want to give them practice spinning out both ways.

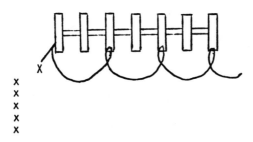

Figure 119

Circle Drill (5-7 men)

One player gets in the middle of a circle about five yards in diameter in a good football position. On a signal from the coach the middle man starts moving his feet, body crouched, pivoting slowly. The coach will call out the name of a man on the outside of the circle, who will rush in facing the defender and deliver a shoulder blow. The defender should step with the foot closest to the rusher and deliver a forearm shiver or shoulder blow to the man. He should play only two or three men, and then get out of the circle, permitting another of the men to move to the middle. Figure 120 illustrates our circle drill.

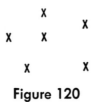

Figure 120

Leverage Drill (8-12 men)

Figure 121 illustrates our Leverage Drill. We have two groups going at the same time in opposite directions. Four blockers are lined up one behind the other, with the defensive man lined up on the outside shoulder of the blocker facing him. On a command by the coach, the defender must play the first blocker with a shiver and the other blockers one at a time with the forearms, shoulders and hands as he retreats and reacts, not permitting himself to be hooked from the outside and blocked in.

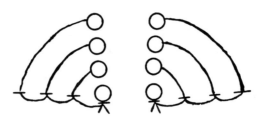

Figure 121

Explode Drill (9 men)

The offensive men will line up with their inside knees on the ground, and the defensive man in the gap between the two offensive men, as illustrated in Figure 122. The defensive player will explode and uncoil on his count with his tail down, head up, and feet moving after bringing them up under him following his initial contact. The coach will give him a hand signal, and the defensive man must spin out properly, ending up in a good football position. It is important for the defensive man to get under the offensive men on his initial charge. We also let the blockers go full speed and teach the defensive man to react from a two-on-one block.

Figure 122

Defensive Reaction Drill (14-18 men)

With the interior linemen from tackle to tackle, we place defensive men head on the center and tackles, as illustrated in Figure 123. A coach will stand behind the defensive men, facing the offensive men, and give hand signals indicating starting count and blocking patterns. The defensive men must react and pursue the football properly.

⊕ COACH

Figure 123

Alabama Wave Drill (8-12 men)

Four men line up facing a coach, in a good football position, feet moving as illustrated in Figure 124. The coach points to his right and the players, using a crossover step, must react in that direction. He then points in another direction and the players stop, plant and start in this direction as quickly as possible. The drill not only is a good conditioner, but teaches quickness, too.

⊕ COACH

Figure 124

Rushing the Passer Drill (12-16 men)

Using the two-men Crowther sled, two defenders explode into the machine with a good hard blow on the snap of the football, spin out laterally, and rush the passer playing through two blockers (X), as indicated in Figure 125. The defensive men must hit with the inside shoulder before spinning out to play through the blockers at the side and rear of the sled.

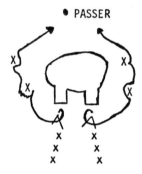

Figure 125

Gauntlet Drill (10-12 men)

We are primarily concerned with the tacklers in this drill. Two rows of jerseys five yards apart is the area the ball carrier (X) is permitted to run with the football. The tacklers (T) are five yards apart, one behind the other. The ball carrier tries to get by the tackler, and the coach checks on the latter's football position—bent at the knees, back straight, hit on the rise, and follow-through. If the coach stands behind the ball carrier, he will be in the best position to observe the tacklers, making certain they do not close their eyes on contact, etc. Figure 126 illustrates our Gauntlet Drill.

Defensive Bucker (4-6 men)

The individual Bucker Drill, not illustrated by diagram, is used when we work in small groups. It teaches the correct form for delivering a blow with the hands, shoulders or forearms. A coach or manager moves the ball to simulate the start of a play, and the defensive man reacts and moves quickly on the sight of the ball.

Figure 126

DRILLS FOR THE LINEBACKERS

The following drills are used to teach individual and team techniques to our linebackers:

All Secondary Drills

Since our linebackers are a part of our defensive secondary, all drills relating to pass defense mentioned and illustrated previously, are also used for our linebackers.

Eye-Opener Drill (8-12 men)

Figure 127 illustrates four large dummies, a line of ball carriers (0) and a line of tacklers (x). The ball carrier either fakes at one hole and goes through the next one, or goes through the first hole trying to beat the tackler. The linebacker tries to keep leverage on the ball carrier, trying to meet him in the hole. The tackler must be careful he does not overrun the ball carrier.

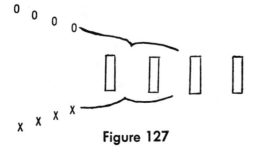

Figure 127

Eye-Closer Drill (12-15 men)

Figure 128 illustrates our Eye-Closer Drill with the offense running its middle attack and the linebackers in particular reacting to every situation they are likely to encounter in a game.

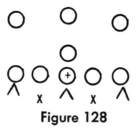

Figure 128

The linebackers also take part in the following drills which I have discussed and illustrated previously:

1. Defensive Bucker Drill.
2. Gauntlet Drill.
3. Middle Drill.
4. Pursuit Drill.
5. Wave Drill.
6. Peel-Off Drill.

DEFENSIVE DRILLS FOR THE TEAM

When we have defensive drills for our team, it is usually three-quarters full speed, or as we commonly refer to it, full speed except for tackling.

We also have drills in which our linemen run half-speed and the defensive secondary, full speed. At times one side of the line will be full speed and the other half-speed. The offense is operating full speed and does not know which side of the defensive line is full speed and which is half-speed.

Our game condition scrimmages are about the only time our entire defensive unit will play full speed, with the exception of full speed goal line defensive scrimmages occasionally. We learn and rehearse our defenses as a team, but seldom scrimmage full speed as a team.

CONCLUSION

We think our drills are functional in nature, and this is why we use them. I cannot see the value of employing drills which are not functional and which do not adhere to the individual and team techniques we will use in a game. We want to drill and rehearse the players in practice the way we want them to perform in a game.

CHAPTER 12

Those Who Stay
Will be Champions

Quitting comes easy for many people. Many do not want to pay the price to be a winner. It requires little effort to be a loser—and anyone who tries can be most successful. The "solid citizens" who finish my "course" will be better men as a result of having stuck it out. The player who sets his mind to do what is required of him in order to be a winner is not only the type of player we are looking for, but he will get the most from the program. Those who stay will be champions and will become winners not only on the football field but in life itself.

Walter D. Wintle's poem about a person's state of mind has a great deal of meaning to it. We have the poem posted in various places throughout our building so our men can read it from time to time. The poem is as follows:

IIt's All in a State of Mind

If you think you are beaten, you are;
If you think you dare not, you won't;
If you like to win, but don't think you can,
It's almost a cinch you won't

If you think you'll lose, you're lost;
For out in the world you'll find
Success begins with a fellow's will;
It's all in a state of mind.

For many a game is lost
Ere even a play is run,
And many a coward fails
Ere even his work is begun.

Think big and your deeds will grow,
Think small and you'll fall behind;
Think that you CAN and you WILL;
It's all in a state of mind.

If you think you are out-classed, you are;
You've got to think high to rise;
You've got to be sure of yourself before
You can ever win a prize.

Life's battles don't always go
To the stronger or faster man,
But sooner or later, the man who wins
Is the fellow who thinks he can.

We must inspire our players to the degree they think and know they are capable of doing what it takes to win. Teaching the men how to accomplish this is extremely gratifying and one of the rewards of coaching.

From time to time, I have been asked, "Coach, what has been your greatest thrill as a football coach?" Trying to single out the "greatest thrill," or even one of my greatest thrills as a coach, is very difficult for me to do. The game of football has been thoroughly rewarding to me.

I can recall many thrills in my coaching days, the great teams at Kentucky that stopped the winning streak at Oklahoma, the 1956 championship team at Texas A&M which started at a training facility in Junction, Texas, the first national championship team here at Alabama in 1961. The great come-from-behind victories at all of the schools, the 315 win that came against Auburn and the final victory against Illinois. All of these are great personal thrills, but the greatest reward in coaching is not winning the big game, but in seeing the young man develop. Seeing him mature not only as a football player but as a successful person. Many of my former players have gone on to become great professional players, professional coaches, college coaches, bankers, lawyers, doctors, school teachers, professional people of all kinds, and I am proud of them all. The real thrill is seeing them reach their potential—not many people do!

> . . . . For out in the world you'll find
> Success begins with a fellow's will;
> It's all in a state of mind. . . .

COACH BRYANT'S
RECORD

The year-by-year head coaching record
of Paul "Bear" Bryant

Year	Team	Record	Year	Team	Record
1945	Maryland 6-2-1		1965	Alabama† 9-1-1	
1946	Kentucky 7-3-0		1966	Alabama..........11-0-0	
1947	Kentucky 8-3-0		1967	Alabama 8-2-1	
1948	Kentucky 5-3-2		1968	Alabama..........8-3-0	
1949	Kentucky 9-3-0		1969	Alabama 6-5-0	
1950	Kentucky..........11-1-0		1970	Alabama 6-5-1	
1951	Kentucky 8-4-0		1971	Alabama..........11-1-0	
1952	Kentucky 5-4-2		1972	Alabama..........10-2-0	
1953	Kentucky 7-2-1		1973	Alabama§ 11-1-0	
1954	Texas A&M.......1-9-0		1974	Alabama..........11-1-0	
1955	Texas A&M.......7-2-1		1975	Alabama..........11-1-0	
1956	Texas A&M.......9-0-1		1976	Alabama 9-3-0	
1957	Texas A&M.......8-3-0		1977	Alabama..........11-1-0	
1958	Alabama 5-4-1		1978	Alabama† 11-1-0	
1959	Alabama 7-2-2		1979	Alabama★........12-0-0	
1960	Alabama 8-1-2		1980	Alabama..........10-2-0	
1961	Alabama★ 11-0-1		1981	Alabama 9-2-1	
1962	Alabama..........10-1-0		1982	Alabama 8-4-0	
1963	Alabama 9-2-0				
1964	Alabama★ 10-1-0		**Total**	................**323-85-17**	

Bear Bryant's career record in 38 years as a head coach.

★ — Denotes final No. 1 ranking in The Associated Press's poll of sportswriters
and broadcasters, and in United Press International's poll of coaches.

† — Denotes final No. 1 ranking in the A.P. poll

§ — Denotes final No. 1 ranking in U.P.I. poll.

BRYANT MILESTONES

Highlights in his head coaching career:

Sept. 1945 — Begins his career at the University of Maryland.

Sept. 28, 1945 — His Maryland Terrapins give him his first head coaching victory by beating Guilford College, 60-6.

Sept. 21, 1946 — Gains his first victory as Kentucky head coach as his Wildcats defeat Mississippi, 20-7.

Feb. 4, 1954 — Named head coach and athletic director at Texas A&M. Blames recurring incidents relating to a basketball scandal at Kentucky for his decision to leave the Wildcats.

Oct. 2, 1954 — Registers his first victory with the Aggies as his squad beats Georgia, 6-0.

May 14, 1955 — His Aggies are hit with a two-year probation by the Southwest Conference for recruiting policy violations. It was to be the last time a Bryant-coached team was placed on probation.

Dec. 3, 1957 — Signs 10-year contract as head coach and athletic director of the University of Alabama.

Oct. 11, 1958 — Notches his first victory with the Crimson Tide, a 29-6 decision over Furman at Tuscaloosa in a night game.

Nov. 7, 1959 — Gets his 100th career victory at Mobile in a 19-7 triumph over Tulane.

Jan. 1, 1962 — Alabama defeats Arkansas, 10-3, in the Sugar Bowl.

Jan. 2, 1962 — Alabama is named national champion in the Associated Press poll for the first time after finishing its first undefeated and untied season with Bryant at the helm.

April 11, 1963 — Files $5 million suit against the Saturday Evening Post for an article charging him and Georgia head coach Wallace Butts with fixing a 1962 game.

April 16, 1963 — A special Legislative committee in Montgomery reports it had found no evidence to support the Saturday Evening Post's charges of game fixing.

Nov. 30, 1964 — Is voted Southeastern Conference Coach of the year.

Jan. 1, 1965 — Alabama loses to Texas, 21-17, in the Orange Bowl.

Jan. 2, 1965 — Despite the loss, the Crimson Tide wins its second AP national championship.

Jan. 1, 1966 — Alabama defeats Nebraska, 39-28, in the Orange Bowl to earn its third AP national championship.

June 20, 1966 — During a coaching clinic at Pepperdine College, he collapses from physical exhaustion and internal bleeding and is taken to a hospital.

Oct. 31, 1968 — Is named all-time Southeastern Conference coach by sports editors and writers.

Sept. 10, 1971 — Collects his 200th career victory as the Tide beats Southern Cal, 17-10, at Los Angeles.

Jan. 13, 1972 — He and Harold Raymond win Coach of the Year honors from the American Football Coaches Association.

Nov. 22, 1973 — Coaches the Crimson Tide to its 500th victory, 21-7 over Louisiana State at Baton Rouge, La.

Jan. 1, 1979 — Alabama defeats Penn. State, 14-7, in the Sugar Bowl.

Jan. 3, 1979 — The Crimson Tide is named national champion in the AP poll for the fourth time.

Dec. 3, 1979 — Is named Coach of the Year.

Jan. 1, 1980 — Alabama defeats Arkansas, 24-9, in the Sugar Bowl to complete its third and final undefeated season under Bryant.

Jan. 2, 1980 — The Crimson Tide is named national champion in the AP poll for the fifth time.

Oct. 5, 1980 — Alabama defeats Kentucky, 45-0, as Bryant becomes the third college football coach to win 300 games.

Nov. 28, 1981 — Passes Amos Alonzo Stagg as the winningest college football coach of all time with his 315th victory in his 37th season, compared with Stagg's 57 seasons.

Jan. 11, 1982 — Receives a special award from the NCAA in recognition of his record-breaking 315th victory.

Nov. 27, 1982 — Alabama drops its regular-season final to Auburn and suffers its first three-game losing streak under Coach Bryant's reign.

Dec. 15, 1982 — Retires from coaching and announces he will remain as athletic director at Alabama.

Dec. 29, 1982 — In his final game, he chalks up victory No. 323 as Alabama defeats Illinois, 21-15, in the Liberty Bowl.

INDEX